the AUTISM NEST model

Second Edition

A Framework for the Inclusive Education of Autistic Students

Edited by

Shirley Cohen, PhD & Allison Graham Brown, MA

The Autism Nest Model

All marketing and publishing rights guaranteed to and reserved by:

FUTURE HORIZONS

(817) 277-0727

www.fhautism.com

The Nest logo was designed by Rex Huang.

ISBN: 978-1-963367-07-2

Music Room

by Rachel Pineda

The music room.
My least favorite place.

The open door stuck out in the hallway like a sore thumb.
Ceiling lights so bright they turned the hallway white.
Tambourines banged tremendously, drums rang relentlessly.
I hated music.

For the first year, I skipped music class.
They were confused, because they did not understand.
They allowed me to sit in another room.
A quiet room. A peaceful room. A better room.
There is just one problem that bothers me.
Everyone else is in the other room. The music room.

The next year, I enter music class.
A rainbow of eight keys catches my eye. A xylophone?
I strike the keys and let their notes enter my ears.
One note, then two notes, then a pretty melody.
They listen. They love it. They want me to play it again.
I want to play that pretty melody again.

Now, the open door welcomes me inside the music room.
I sit in the corner, facing away from the bright white lights.
Many instruments synchronize to form a lively symphony.
I love music.

The music room.
My favorite place.

Rachel was born and raised in Queens, NY, and is a proud Nest graduate. Rachel worked as a tutor for college students with learning disabilities.
Rachel graduated from Queens College with a BA in Psychology.

TABLE OF CONTENTS

PART III: Looking Back Across 20 Years of Nest

FOREWORD

As the deputy chancellor for Inclusive and Accessible Learning for the New York City Public Schools, I am honored to write this foreword for the second edition of *The Autism Nest Model: A Framework for the Inclusive Education of Autistic Students*. The Nest program holds a special place in the landscape of inclusive education, not only for its groundbreaking approach but also for its unwavering commitment to evolving with the needs of our students.

The success of the Nest program is a testament to the tireless dedication of its founders, Dorothy Siegel and Shirley Cohen; Kristie Patten's partnership at New York University; and the leaders of the NYU Nest Support Project, both past and present, including Aaron Lanou and Allison Graham Brown, among many others. Thousands of NYC Public Schools educators and administrators have been influenced by the program's philosophy of inclusive practices, empathy, and incorporating feedback from individuals with lived experiences. Families and advocates recognize the benefits and success of this program not only for our autistic learners but for all students. Together, educators, administrators, families, and advocates have iteratively improved the model to ensure we are creating classrooms and school environments where every student thrives.

I remain in awe of the scalability of this program. In New York City, the largest school system in the country, Nest began as a pilot program in two classrooms at PS 32 in Brooklyn, galvanized by the passion of Dorothy Siegel. As is so often the case, the Nest concept was driven by a mother who was unrelentingly committed to meeting the needs of her autistic child, Samuel, and other children like him. Two decades later, in 2024, Nest exists in 88 schools and over 410 classrooms. Its students are graduating high school in four years at a rate of 95 percent. Students in Nest are outpacing their peers with journeys that often include first playdates and the forging of true and lasting friendships, thanks to the social and communication supports inherent to the Nest program.

What makes the Nest program truly extraordinary is its holistic approach to inclusion and universal design. By prioritizing the needs of both autistic and non-autistic students, the program creates a supportive ecosystem where every learner can thrive.

From collaborative structures to sensory-safe environments, every aspect of the Nest program is designed to foster growth, understanding, and empowerment for all students. Principals often say, "The Nest program transformed how teaching and learning take place across my entire school."

I extend my deepest gratitude to all those who have contributed to the development of the Nest program over the years. Your dedication and passion have transformed the lives of countless students and families, leaving an indelible mark on the landscape of special education in New York City and beyond.

With warm regards,

Christina Foti
June 2024

PREFACE

The ASD Nest program grew out of a dream that Dorothy Siegel had had for a long time. Her dream was to create a program in neighborhood NYC public schools that would include autistic children and serve them well. Dorothy needed a partner to help her turn that dream into reality, and she chose me, Shirley Cohen, to be that partner.

Once Dorothy decided that I was the right one, there was no escaping. I was hooked and have been hooked since that day in 2001 when I finished a presentation called "Helping Parents Look at Alternative Approaches to Autistic Spectrum Disorders" and Dorothy came up to me and said something like, "Can I talk to you about an idea I have?"

During the next two years the ASD Nest program was conceived, and in fall 2003, the first two ASD Nest classes opened in Brooklyn. Something good blossomed from Dorothy's dream, something that has enabled many children and their families to live happier/healthier lives.

The first edition of *The ASD Nest Model* was published in 2013, ten years after a program based on that model was conceived, pilot tested, and implemented in a New York City public school. This second edition adds the story of what we learned and did during those intervening years and how the original model evolved since the first book was written. This is also a story of the dedicated teachers, speech therapists, occupational therapists, social workers, and school administrators who made this program work for many children, helping them reach their unique potential and live happier and healthier lives.

Families are part of this story too. We reached out to them, and they responded. Their children showed us what frightened them, what angered them, what they loved, and how we could help them. Most children in our program met or exceeded the hopes of their families, and virtually all children progressed above earlier expectations. Some are now college graduates, others are college students or are about to enter college, and some are high school graduates who have embarked on vocational/career paths. You will learn more about them as you read on.

Much has changed in the past ten years in the field of autism, and so has this model. For example, the subtitle of the 2013 version of this book referred to "higher functioning children with autism spectrum disorders," but we no longer refer to children as higher functioning or not. The ASD Nest program begins at the kindergarten level, and over the years, we have seen some amazing transformations in our students. We would have been sorely remiss in continuing to view students through the prism of higher functioning or its absence, and that terminology is also no longer in frequent use in the wider field.

The ASD Nest is not a static model. Throughout its evolution, we have maintained the original foundation and attempted to reflect its objectives, structures, supports, and other strategic elements while also responding and adapting to changing needs in society, education, and the field of autism. The model has also evolved in response to our students' moves from elementary to middle and high schools that have different administrative structures and expectations, as well as to the students becoming adolescents with different developmental needs, interests, and passions. Our culture has also changed. While we continue to refer to "children with autism spectrum disorders" when parents or individuals prefer that terminology, we use the term "autistic students" in our evolved model. This term is gaining support in the broader autism field and is strongly supported by self-advocates. Finally, our model has benefited greatly from the thinking of autistic self-advocates, which has had a profound impact on our understanding of autistic students and our work.

—Shirley Cohen, PhD, 2024

ACKNOWLEDGMENTS

We are grateful to many people for supporting the early work of Dorothy Siegel and Shirley Cohen in bringing the ASD Nest program from idea to reality. New York University's Institute for Education and Social Policy was the first home for this project. Dorothy's early work, in particular, was supported by Norman Fruchter, director of the Institute, whose early nurturance and guidance were critical to germinating the Nest idea into a flesh-and-bones program. Dean Mary Brabeck of the Steinhardt School was encouraging and supportive.

From 2002–2004, the development of the Nest program model was facilitated by a New York City Department of Education planning team established by District 15 superintendent Carmen Farina. The planning team members were Ronni Ableman, Ruth Blankiet, David Cohen, Sherry Koslov, Ann Marie Lettieri-Baker, and Steven Rosen. After becoming deputy chancellor of the New York City Department of Education in 2004, Carmen Farina introduced the Nest Model in all five boroughs of New York City. Linda Wernikoff and Terry Feuer of the Department of Education's Office of Special Education Initiatives played critical roles in that rollout.

From 2004 to the present, the NYC Department of Education, now called NYC Public Schools (NYCPS), provided annual funding to NYU for program development, facilitation, and support. Early grants from the FAR Fund, Independence Community Foundation, Overbrook Foundation, and Tides Foundation supported early planning and model development.

Hunter College received funding from the NYC Department of Education for staff training and support during most of that period. Hunter also received funding from the New York State Education Department for the development of a program to train teachers of students with autism, which became the foundation of pre-service training for the new staff of Nest.

Over the two decades of Nest's existence, several people at the NYC Department of Education's central office were essential to Nest's success: Kate Dolan-Cheney, Christina Foti, Michelle Netzler, Corinne Rello-Anselmi, and Suzanne Sanchez. Simply put, they believed in Nest and did what needed to be done to make it successful.

Of the hundreds of teachers, principals, and therapists whose work contributed so much to the Nest Model, we would like to individually acknowledge two extraordinary Nest teachers, Lauren Hough Williams and Aaron Lanou. After moving to NYU, they continually refined the Nest Model and developed the excellent professional development and support mechanisms that sustain the model today. Aaron also led the initial team, which helped Denmark adapt and adopt the Nest Model to the Danish education system. Today Lauren is executive director of PINE, NYU's inclusion training program available to schools and districts across the country.

Susan Ehlerman is the brilliant speech and language pathologist whose understanding of autistic children led her to create and continually rethink Social Development Intervention, the therapeutic heart of the Nest Model. When Kristie Patten arrived at NYU in 2007, she added the crucial occupational therapy perspective to the model. Since 2013, she has been the principal investigator of the Nest Support Project at NYU. Since 2021, Allison Graham Brown has been the executive director for the Nest Support Project. Under her leadership, the number of Nest schools doubled and the model continued to evolve while maintaining fidelity to the original Nest Model.

We would also like to express our appreciation to three Hunter College professionals–Jamie Bleiweiss, Angela Mousakites, and Donia Fahim–who worked closely with Shirley Cohen during the early years of the ASD Nest program to provide training as both course instructors and field consultants at participating schools. Jamie, in particular, greatly enriched the Nest program through her extensive understanding and experience in implementing positive behavior supports.

In the earliest days of Nest, every school that embraced the Nest program contributed in important ways to its development. We offer special thanks to the principals and staff of our pioneering Nest schools—PS 4 on Staten Island, PS 32 in Brooklyn, PS 112 in Manhattan, PS 165 and PS 186 in Queens, and PS 396 in the Bronx—for helping to blaze a path toward excellence in serving autistic students. Every day, hundreds of New York City public school educators, principals, and therapists work diligently, in partnership with Nest families, to understand and educate Nest students. We are grateful for their dedication to creating bright futures for these autistic students.

A NOTE ON LANGUAGE

In the first edition of this book, the language used was reflective of the terms being used in education, diagnostics, and the autism community at that time. Those terms included ASD, Aspergers, and person-first language (ex: a person with autism, a child on the spectrum). However, as the field evolved, so did the language and terms used. Over time, much of the disability advocate community has shifted to identify-first language: autistic person (child or student). Therefore, in this edition of the book, we will primarily use identity-first language. However, we will use some person-first language across the second edition to reflect an inclusive approach and acknowledgment that how each individual is referred to is up to that person.

Part 1 of this book presents the conceptualization, development, and implementation of the original ASD Nest Model between 2001 and 2012. Part 2 presents the current, evolved model with a focus on the period from 2013 through 2023, and Part 3 looks back at the past twenty years of the model and then takes a look into the future. The reader will note differences in terminology between Part 1 and the two other parts, specifically changing from ASD Nest program to Autism Nest program. The evolution of the model led to those changes.

PART I
Foundations

CHAPTER 1

Beginnings: The Why, What, When, and How of the ASD Nest Program

Dorothy Siegel and Shirley Cohen

Dorothy

"Stop the Car! There's something I *have* to do! We need to talk about it!" It was the summer of 1999, and I was traveling with my family from Denver to Santa Fe. Temple Grandin's new book, *Thinking in Pictures*, was in my lap, resting on a map of Colorado. I had just reached the part of the book where Temple stated her belief that "early intervention in a good program can enable about 50 percent of autistic children to be enrolled in a normal first grade" and "their ability to live a normal life will be improved" (1995, 49–50). I knew the grim reality, and it was quite different. At that point in time, very few autistic children were being educated in general education classes, and those who were rarely did well: many had limited communication skills, their academic skills were spotty, and social relations with peers were often absent or inappropriate and problematic. How could Temple's statement possibly be right?

My own son, Sam, who was seventeen at that time, was managing to achieve academic success, but that required a huge effort by the entire family and an education at two excellent publicly funded private special education schools. I had spent the first dozen or so years of Sam's life digging myself out of despair and devoting myself to figuring out what seemed to be the problem with my child, what it was that he needed, and how to find or create whatever that was. Along the way, I learned a lot about special education, the New York City public school system, and autism.

In 1989 I was elected to Community School Board 15 in Brooklyn, one of the thirty-two semi-autonomous New York City community school boards that shared responsibility with the central administration for educating over one million students. I had a lot of questions. From my position on the school board, I opened up a local and citywide conversation about special education, posing these questions:

- Why were the students identified as needing special education services usually segregated from their general education peers?
- What structures, attitudes, policies, and practices were responsible for the generally poor outcomes of students receiving special education?
- How could we reconceptualize both special and general education to maximize successful outcomes for students with special needs?
- How could we make that kind of change happen and then institutionalize it?

My Community School District 15 colleagues and I launched a task force on special education. We studied the history and theories of special education, explored the inner workings of the special education system, held numerous public discussions, and did some honest soul-searching. The task force's motto was, "Children are more alike than they are different and should be educated together, whenever possible." In the end, following the Task Force's recommendations, the District 15 superintendent, Bill Casey, embraced and instituted several changes the task force recommended that changed special education provision across the district and, eventually, citywide. One change was the creation and replication of a collaborative co-teaching model, which eventually became a popular form of inclusion (renamed Integrated Co-Teaching or ICT) first in District 15 and then throughout New York City's public schools (NYCPS). The ICT model also served as a forerunner of the structure of the ASD Nest Model.

In 1995, I joined the Institute for Education and Social Policy at New York University as a policy analyst and researcher. My first assignment was to serve as a key consultant for a study and report commissioned by New York City schools chancellor Ramon Cortines: *Focus on Learning: Reorganizing General and Special Education in the New York City Public Schools*. The report expanded on many of the ideas my District 15 colleagues and I had developed, and in the late 1990s, *Focus on Learning* became a blueprint for special education reform in New York City.

Four years later, as I read Temple Grandin's book *Thinking in Pictures*. (1995) her words stirred me anew. I realized that she was right. I had learned from my work as a school board member, special education advocate, and, more recently, policy analyst at NYU, that most disabled children, including children with autism, could be helped greatly by targeted early education strategies. I saw how much this had benefited my own son.

I also knew from my ten years of trying to understand and improve the public education system that the current state of education for autistic students within New York City was not optimal, and that changing the system to improve educational opportunities and outcomes would not be easy in such a huge institution. I did not know how to accomplish this task, but I felt compelled to try. I realized that this was an "inside-outside" task. That is, it required the joining of an insider's knowledge and expertise with the leverage of someone who worked "outside" the system. My experiences with, and in-depth studies of, the school system, combined with my research perch at NYU, made me the kind of "inside-outside" person who *might* be able to accomplish that task. From my work on the District 15 Special Education task force, I had learned what good special education looks like, paired with having a parent's knowledge of what autistic students need. As an education policy analyst at NYU, I had the time and opportunity to study the field of school reform. I understood what type of school reform was possible and how to scale up such reforms. Most importantly, I also had access to many top-notch educators in both public and private schools (especially The Summit School in Queens, NY) who were selflessly willing to help me figure out how to improve the education of autistic students in the public school system.

I was reluctant to take on such a gargantuan task; however, as I read Temple's words on that day in 1999, I realized that I could not refuse her call. It was time to talk with my husband about this "something" that I just *had* to do. As usual, he provided great insight and support; he was as excited as I about the possibility of positively altering the life prospects of autistic students. He said, "Go for it!"

That fall, and into winter 2000, I invited three of my former District 15 colleagues plus a retired superintendent of District 75 (according to the NYCPS, District 75 provides highly specialized instructional support for students with significant challenges) to my house for a discussion and a meal of baba ganoush, hummus, tabbouleh, and stuffed grape leaves, accompanied by red wine. All of us were very proud of the special education programs and practices District 15 had created in the '90s and the level of excellence demanded for every student therein. Informal analyses showed that students with special needs in District 15, especially those in the new inclusion (ICT) settings, performed better academically than similarly situated students in other community school districts and better than District 15 students with special needs in years past. The Central Board of Education noticed these improved outcomes as well and decided to adopt District 15's ICT inclusion model across the city. In 1999 or 2000, the ICT model was formally included on the NYCPS's "Continuum of Services."

"So," I asked my District 15 colleagues, "we know many students do well in District 15's inclusion classes, but tell me, in particular, how do autistic students in those classes do?" "Their parents are happy," one replied. "Of course their parents are happy," I said. "For the first time, their children are being included in the same classrooms as their neighbors' children. That alone makes parents happy. But I want to know how the students are really doing. Are they learning? Are they coping with their classroom's social demands? Are they able to move on to higher grades with their typically developing peers?" Silence. Then one colleague spoke up, "Well, actually, they are not doing as well as we would like. They often wind up in a more restrictive placement sooner or later." "Why?" I pressed. "Because we don't know what they need that's any different from the needs of other students with special needs." OK. Now we're getting somewhere. We had identified the problem: *We don't know what the autistic students need.* "So let's read a book," I said, "and figure that out."

Over the next few months, our group met three more times, always over baba ganoush and wine. We read and discussed Shirley Cohen's book, *Targeting Autism: What We Know, Don't Know and Can Do to Help Young Children with Autism Spectrum Disorders* (1998). A professor of special education at Hunter College, Shirley was widely regarded as an expert on the education of young children with ASD. We found her book to be truly enlightening, and we began to understand why the otherwise-successful District 15 inclusion classes were not so successful for autistic students. But we still struggled to understand what these students needed and what would work for them. I had to find this Shirley Cohen person and talk with her. I had to convince her to become my partner in this quest.

CHAPTER 1

Shirley

In 1993, I began receiving telephone calls in my office in the Special Education Department of Hunter College from parents of young children diagnosed with autism. These parents wanted me to identify Hunter College students who would work in their homes to help implement an intensive applied behavior analysis (ABA) intervention approach. At that point in time, I was only mildly familiar with this approach and did not look very favorably on it. From my background and framework in developmental psychology and early childhood education, I viewed it as mechanistic, restrictive, and somewhat punitive. I did not know that the model of ABA developed by O. Ivar Lovaas—The Young Autism Project model—was seen by many parents of children with autism as the only way to "save" their children. Some parents berated me for not knowing more about the "great outcomes" from this approach and for not supporting it strongly in multiple ways. I had begun my special education teaching career in the 1960s, working for three years in a treatment and research center for children with autism. That had been the most powerful learning experience I had ever had, although I was dismayed by the huge gap in the knowledge base on how to teach such children during that time period. Basically, I had to create my own approach and educational intervention strategies. Some of my students were helped a great deal; others made little progress. Here it was more than thirty years later, and I recognized that something new and important had taken place. I switched back to a heavy focus on autism instead of working cross-categorically in special education and immersed myself in what was happening.

A few years later, I participated in a meeting of the advocacy committee of the New York Autism Network, a state-funded three-year project, where I met this bright, committed, and outspoken person, Dorothy Siegel. A short while later, in early 2001, Dorothy attended a conference presentation I gave on informing parents of children with autism about issues and options. After my presentation, she asked to meet with me. What followed was more than a year's worth of very long telephone conversations during which we conceptualized the ASD Nest program. I had one major concern at that time: I feared that we would spend years developing and implementing a good program that would then be spread widely without sufficient training and support, and with some of its core components diluted or missing, at which point the program would no longer be effective. I had seen that happen before, and I didn't think we would be able to prevent that from happening to the ASD Nest program. Dorothy offered me a deal: I would decide what had to be done, and Dorothy would figure out how to do it and make sure the Department of Education did so, whatever that required. That was our pact.

The Problem: No Appropriate Program for My Child

By 2000, it became clear that there was a severe shortage of educational programs designed for school-age students with autism. Many students had good early intervention and preschool services. However, when they entered the public school system at age five, they fell off a metaphorical cliff, into a system that provided no appropriate programs for them. This led to inappropriate school placements, frequent changes in placement, and a lack of support that virtually ensured poor educational experiences.

Cases in Point 1998–1999

CHILD 1: JAY. A distraught mother called Shirley. She didn't understand what was going on in the school system. Her six-year-old son had been in kindergarten the previous year. Near the end of that year, she was asked to come to a meeting at his school and was told that her son would not be able to move on to first grade the next fall: He was not ready for first grade. Instead, it was recommended that he repeat kindergarten in a class that would have two teachers, one of them a special education teacher. Jay's mother agreed, and Jay began kindergarten for the second time in the fall in a co-teaching class with twenty-four other children. About six weeks into the fall semester, the school called again. Even though there were two teachers in Jay's classroom, she was told that there were too many students in the class. Jay was not doing well; he needed a smaller class.

This time the school recommended a special education class with twelve students, a special education teacher, and a paraprofessional. Again Jay's mother agreed. Jay's IEP was revised, and he entered the special education class. A few weeks later, Jay's mother was called to the school again. This time, the school wanted her son to be seen by a psychiatrist and moved to a different school. At that point, she said, "No more." She had given up hope that the public school system could meet her son's needs. She arranged for an evaluation of Jay at a hospital clinic, which identified him as having Asperger syndrome. Soon thereafter, she engaged an attorney to fight for a private school placement because she no longer trusted the public school system. Jay's mother won that fight. This mother believed that the public school system had wasted almost two years of her son's school years.

CHILD 2: BEN. Ben had been diagnosed with autistic disorder before age three, at which point his parents arranged for intensive behavioral intervention plus speech therapy. Ben made excellent progress and began attending a nursery school program for half days with support from an aide while continuing to receive behavioral intervention for the other half of the day. By age six, Ben had a very high nonverbal IQ and enjoyed interacting with adults and some children, but his language was still below the expected level for his age.

His parents wanted Ben to enter a first-grade class in the fall with support from a teaching assistant trained by their in-home therapy program coordinator; they also wanted his classroom teacher to receive training on ASD. The teaching assistant was not assigned until a month of school had gone by, and no training on ASD had been provided for the teacher. Ben could not follow the back-and-forth communication going on in this class of almost twenty-five students and got lost during the first month. He did not do well during that school year. His parents felt that the year would have been totally wasted were it not for the nurturing provided by three six-year-old girls in his class who recognized that Ben needed some special support. The following year Ben was moved to a special education school where the instruction and support from professionals was excellent, although it meant hours of travel each day for this young boy, and there were no typically developing peers in his class or school.

These two students are examples of the many autistic students who lacked an educational home in the New York City school system, students who may have difficulty coping with change and unexpected events, who may be easily overwhelmed by the movements and sounds of active learning in large groups, who might not follow much of the back-and-forth of discussions because of the extra time they need to process language, who may not be aware of how they are affecting others, who are often easy targets for bullying, who may not know how to make friends even when they want to, and who may have difficulty reading facial expressions.

Existing programs fell into three categories: co-teaching (ICT) with large class registers (including up to 40 percent of students with IEPs) that overwhelm autistic students; smaller self-contained classes with a special education teacher and a paraprofessional, neither of whom might have had any training on understanding and working with autistic students; or a mainstream class with a general education teacher aided by a one-to-one paraprofessional.

None of these were good matches for many autistic students. The NYC public schools needed a new program model that would provide good teaching aimed specifically at the areas in which these students have great difficulty, such as understanding social contexts and classroom expectations and developing the awareness and skills to navigate them; smaller class sizes; teachers who know when and how to provide needed support; and a classroom culture of understanding, acceptance, and support from teachers and peers. That is what the program that became the ASD Nest aimed to provide.

Engaging the Public School System

Community School District 15 in western Brooklyn was the best place to start such a program because of Dorothy's work on inclusion in that district as a member of its Community School Board and the relationships she had developed over the years in that role. One of those relationships was a long-standing friendship with Carmen Farina, the new superintendent of the district who had been a teacher and staff developer in District 15 for many years and most recently served ten years as the principal of an elementary school in Manhattan. During that time, she also had come to know Dorothy's son Sam—his history, his strengths, and his challenges—and was disturbed that there was no program for students like Sam in District 15 schools. Had it not been for Sam's acceptance at a private special education school, he would have had to go to a District 75 program for students with autism. While Sam's support needs were high, he was also very bright, and District 75 had no program that could match his academic needs.

Dorothy knew that starting any new program required a strong rationale based on an unmet need. But it also required a fierce champion whose stature in the school system would enable her to propose a new service model. Dorothy went into full advocacy mode to ensure that Carmen Farina, who was such a person, would work with us to develop and sponsor our new program model. Carmen turned out to be a natural ally. She strongly favored the idea of moving autistic students into local schools rather than requiring them to attend a District 75 program.

By late 2001, we had the four ingredients necessary to start our new program model: a demonstrably strong educational need that was not being adequately addressed by any other program, an advocate with excellent knowledge of the school system and deep roots in the local school district (Dorothy), an expert in autism education with a graduate program focused on that area (Shirley), and a high-level school administrator who had the interest and ability to establish a new program model (Carmen).

The vision that Dorothy and I had created for serving autistic students in New York City neighborhood schools began to look as if it might be realized. We mapped out a sequence of activities that would need to be implemented on the road toward achieving that vision.

A Study Group Is Established: 2001–2002

Starting a new program model necessitated the support of all key players in District 15. Therefore, in early 2002, Carmen created a District 15 study group on educating students with autism as a vehicle for involving key district personnel and gaining their advice and support. Included in the study group were the district's director of special education, chair of the committee on special education, director of speech services, director of guidance, special education supervisor overseeing the district's inclusion program, the parent of an autistic student who resided in the district, the principal, the parent association president, the psychologist of the school Carmen selected as the future pilot site, and the director of a neighborhood preschool that was a feeder program for the pilot school.

Shirley and Dorothy designed and ran a series of five monthly workshops with the members of the District 15 study group. A major theme of the workshops was the conclusion in the 2001 report of the National Research Council, *Educating Children with Autism*, that "education, both directly of children, and of parents and teachers, is currently the primary form of treatment of autism" (p. 12). So if education was the primary form of treatment for autism, what did that education involve? What were the characteristics of children with autism and the best thinking and evidence on educational intervention practices for such children? What examples were there of good practices in those New York City schools, mostly private, that were successfully educating autistic children? What structures did a program model need to help autistic students succeed in New York City public schools?

Outside experts and District 15 personnel made presentations to the study group, along with Shirley Cohen, Dorothy Siegel, and Sam Abram, Dorothy's son. Because the study group participants wanted a better understanding of the school experiences, perspectives, and development of older students with autism, they asked Sam, then a high school student, to speak about what had been most difficult for him as a child and what he felt had helped him the most.

Questions, contributions by other study group members, and discussions took up a good part of each half-day meeting. In order to expand the participants' knowledge base, we established a lending library of books on ASD. Books were exchanged and discussed at each meeting. Visits to private school programs with good reputations for serving autistic students were also arranged. Finally, the group discussed the feasibility of implementing a program for autistic students in a District 15 school that was derived from various existing models and best practices.

One of the early decisions made by the study group was that whatever model they selected for implementation had to involve authentic inclusion, which was the major element missing from the good nonpublic school programs that the group had visited, and was a principle to which District 15 had a strong commitment. Another element with strong support was the necessity of a solid training program for teachers and therapists who would work in the program. Fortunately, the New York State Education Department had just awarded Hunter College a grant to develop and implement such training under Shirley's direction, and new staff of the ASD program could be required to take that training. Furthermore, it was decided that only certified teachers and related service providers would work with students in the program. Paraprofessionals or other aides would not be used in this new model.

In June 2002, the study group concluded its work with a strong recommendation to Superintendent Farina that District 15 develop a program model to be piloted in grades

K–2 in one school, starting in September 2003. The 2002–03 school year would be used to delineate the specific elements of that model and to make arrangements for its implementation. The study group also recommended that a District 15 ASD Planning Committee be established to oversee the program's development and implementation.

The goal of the proposed ASD Planning Committee was clear: to develop and implement a model that would help autistic students function comfortably and successfully in their classrooms and communities. The mission for the new program model was also clear: **to create the best possible public school model for autistic students—a model that could be scaled up to public schools in every New York City neighborhood.**

Carmen agreed. Two small grants from private foundations supported the development of the original Nest program model. Those funds were used to pay for costs associated with study group meetings, the planning process, and program startup. Additional grants from 2003 through 2006 supported the development and implementation of workshops for families, as well as participation by ASD Nest staff in conferences on autism held in the greater New York area. Thus, funding by private foundations enriched both program development and professional development. Our vision had moved another giant step toward realization.

The Planning Year: 2002–2003

The District 15 ASD Planning Committee consisted of a small group of professionals drawn from the members of the study group—the district's director of special education, chair of the district committee on special education (CSE), and director of speech services, along with the principal of the pilot school and special education inclusion supervisor assigned to that school. Both Dorothy and Shirley served on the planning committee as well. The district's CSE chair was responsible for identifying district students classified as autistic who might benefit from the new program.

Two models were selected for piloting. One of them, which we initially called a Micro-Inclusion Kindergarten, was derived from the LEAP model (Learning Experiences: An Alternative Program for Preschoolers and Parents), a nationally validated private preschool program for autistic students (Strain and Bovey 2008). LEAP is an inclusion model with a small class size and a ratio of two typically developing students to each autistic student. The model had two teachers and an assistant teacher in each classroom plus a speech therapist who served two LEAP classes, as well as a family service coordinator who worked with parents.

The second model selected for piloting in the first grade ASD classroom was based loosely on a program being implemented in the Seattle school system that served students with autism. The Seattle model took the form of a special education class with seven students, a teacher, and an aide, with students from that class participating "in mainstream classes as much as possible, sometimes with the support of the aide." Students worked in the special education classroom "only when they needed to work on certain skills" (Fine 2001).

Two models, rather than one, were selected for piloting because we were not sure that the preschool model derived from LEAP would work as well with kindergarten-age children in a public elementary school as it had with preschoolers in a private setting. While the Seattle model seemed appropriate for older elementary-age children in a public school setting, only anecdotal data were available about the effectiveness of that model.

The Pilot Project: 2003–2005

In 2003 the two models for the ASD program were piloted at PS 32, the Brooklyn school selected by Superintendent Farina. In late spring and summer of that year, the district committee on special education selected students with autism for the kindergarten and first grade pilot classes, teachers and other staff were trained at Hunter College, visits to the homes of each child were made by two staff members, and students and parents visited their new classrooms.

The major structural elements of the Micro-Inclusion Kindergarten model were the 2:1 ratio of typically developing students to autistic students for a total register of twelve students; two teachers, one of whom had special education certification; the use of peer models; and the use of the district's academic curriculum for kindergarten with adaptations and additions to meet the special needs of the students with autism.

The other model was implemented with five autistic students at the first-grade level. While loosely based on the Seattle program, this program was implemented with two teachers, one with special education certification, but no paraprofessional aides. One of the teachers accompanied pairs of students when they went from their home base classroom to another classroom of typically developing students.

The Micro-Inclusion Kindergarten model utilized the standard academic curriculum of the local district and school, with adaptations as needed for autistic students to access the curriculum. Additionally, we recognized a need for the classroom to have an expanded focus on developing relationships, supporting social/communication competence, developing self-regulation, and reducing interfering behaviors. Based on this, we developed a rudimentary intervention framework shown in figure 1.1, called Cornerstones of the Micro-Inclusion Kindergarten Program (Cohen 2006).

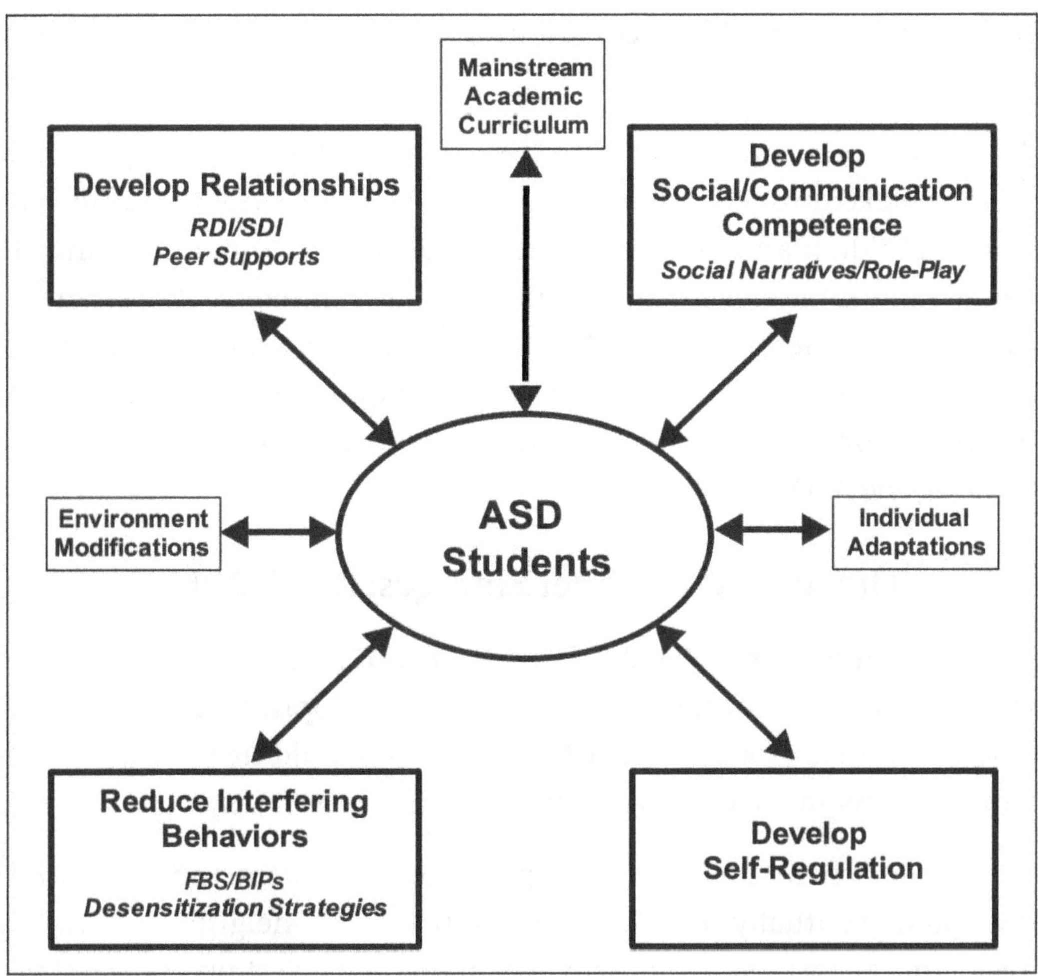

FIGURE 1.1. Based on Cornerstones of the Micro-Inclusion Kindergarten Program, Cohen, 2006, page 18

Across the first pilot year, it became clear that the Seattle-based model was not working well for the first-grade autistic students. For one thing, the Seattle model required autistic students to be mainstreamed into general education classrooms with typically developing students. However, the general education classes in this pilot school, like most schools in the NYC public school system (known at the time as the NYC Department of Education), had a high percentage of students with special needs, some of whom had IEPs or were being considered for special education. In addition, general education class sizes in the pilot school, again like that of many NYC Public Schools (NYCPS), was already high, and having so many students in the classroom could create a significant sensory impact and a less-than-ideal environment for social development.

During that same year the students in the Micro-Inclusion Kindergarten did well. Parents were happy with their child's overall progress and increased social interactions with peers.

The ASD Planning Committee decided to continue to pilot both program models for a second year to make sure that what we saw happening was not primarily a function of one group of children and one set of teachers. As It turned out, it wasn't. The Seattle-based model did no better in the second year with different classes and different teachers, whereas the Micro-Inclusion Kindergarten model again produced more communication and socialization in students as well as happier parents. The pilot program ended after that second year, with a slightly modified version of the Micro-Inclusion model becoming the ASD Nest program.

The ASD Nest Model Emerges: 2005–2012

A model began to emerge in 2004–2005 based on the Micro-Inclusion Kindergarten pilot. From that point forward, our focus was on developing an educational model based on the Micro-Inclusion Kindergarten pilot that would help autistic students be successful in mainstream settings in their school and community.

Our intention was to create a public school program for autistic students, based on this model, that could eventually be implemented in all NYC neighborhoods. We called this new program the ASD Nest program. The name ASD Nest was selected because it connotes a small, nurturing environment in which autistic students could feel safe and

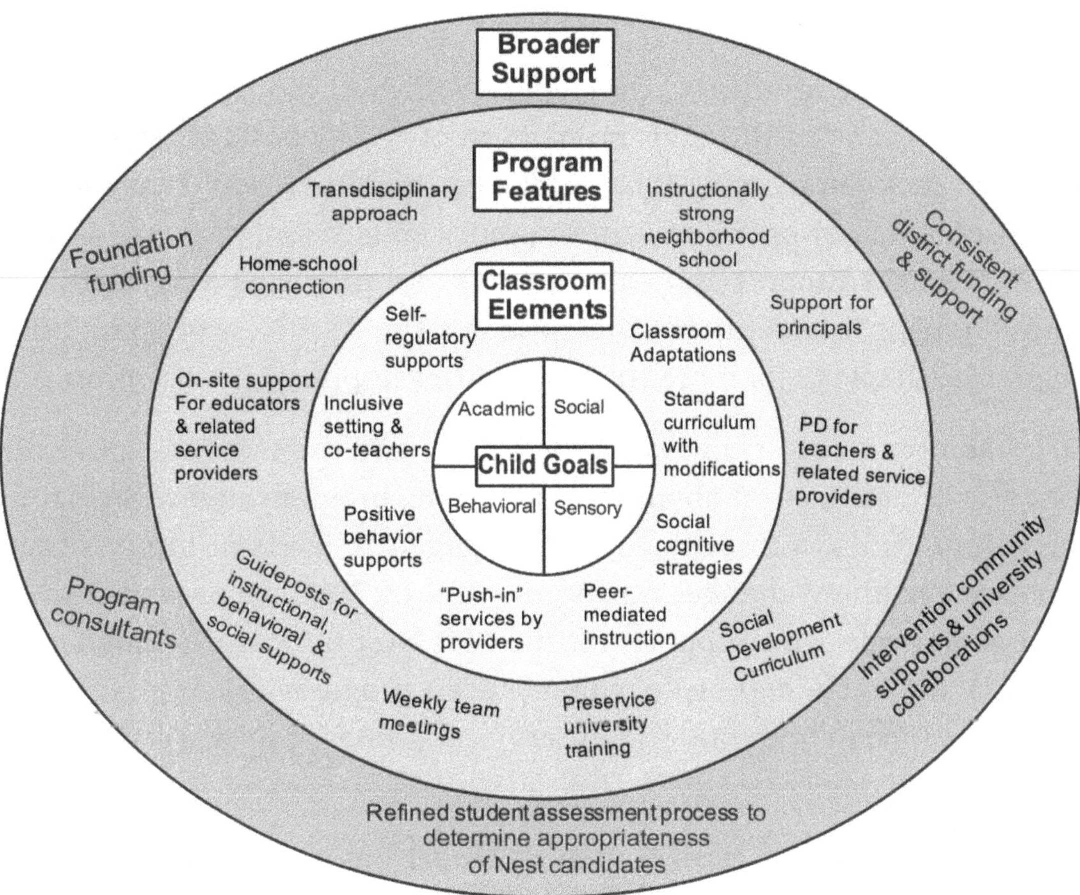

FIGURE 1.2. The ASD Nest Model, (n.d.)

flourish. The Nest *Model* refers to the comprehensive package of philosophical tenets, structures, and strategies and the term Nest *program* is used to refer to the application of the model in schools.

In March 2004, Carmen Farina was appointed deputy chancellor of the NYCPS. She called Dorothy into her office and told her that she wanted to spread the Nest program beyond District 15 and create a replication plan to do so. Accordingly, Dorothy developed a plan based on the research done by Cynthia E. Coburn on scaling up school reform models, "Rethinking Scale: Moving Beyond Numbers to Deep and Lasting Change" (Coburn 2003). Understanding and implementing Coburn's findings were, and continue to be, essential in successfully and sustainably replicating the Nest Model.

The ASD Nest program was launched at two additional public schools, PS 4 on Staten Island and PS 112 in Manhattan. Early Nest schools started with two Nest kindergarten classes. Over time, we continued to develop the ASD Nest Model. In 2007, we concretized the program elements through the creation of "Guideposts for Staff of ASD Nest programs," and an accompanying checklist (Cohen and Bleiweiss). That checklist used an organizational framework of prevention, replacement, and response derived from the positive behavior support approach. In 2008 we produced a parallel document, "Social Development Intervention Guideposts for the ASD Nest program" (Brennan and Hough). See chapter 9 for more about Social Development Intervention.

By 2010, it had become clear that we needed to expand the two Guideposts and integrate both sets of practices. At about the same time, program staff recognized that it would be helpful to use a three-tier system to organize levels of intervention intensity. Work on both these changes was begun, and in 2011, we produced the "Three Tier Model of Strategies and Supports for the ASD Nest program" (Hough et al.) and "Expanded Classroom Guideposts for the ASD Nest program" (Bleiweiss et al.). These documents were used in both pre- and in-service training for several years. See chapter 3 for more about this.

While the ASD Nest Model has been continuously refined, its core features have remained intact. Those features consist of the following:

- *Reduced class size:* twelve students at the kindergarten level, sixteen students in grades one through three; up to twenty students in grades four and five.
- *Co-teaching:* two classroom teachers, one certified in special education and one in general early childhood or childhood education, plus a cluster teacher, licensed in special education, who supports children during special subjects and instructional lunch.
- *Targeted goal areas:* communication, social understanding and social development, self-regulation and coping, selected academic skills as needed by individual students.
- *Use of supports delineated in Nest Model materials:* resources created for the model that outline strategies for implementation.
- *Transdisciplinary team approach:* teams consist of speech-language pathologists (SLPs), occupational therapists (OTs), social workers or guidance counselors, principal or assistant principal, classroom co-teachers, cluster teacher; weekly meetings held after school for one to 1.5 hours for case conferences, professional development and team planning.

- *Preservice training:* conducted the summer before new staff join the program through graduate-level courses on autism, behavioral theory and its applications, and a variety of other intervention approaches and strategies, offered at Hunter College and later at NYU.
- *In-service training:* ongoing professional development workshops provided across the school year on foundational and novel topics and strategies in the field of autism and education.
- *Discipline-specific in-service seminars:* novel seminar series provided across the year for teachers, cluster teachers, speech therapists, occupational therapists, social workers/guidance counselors, and administrators.
- *Ongoing site support:* program consultants working for New York University and for several initial years for Hunter College provide support on a regular basis, more intensively during the first two years of the program; meetings with principals about administrative matters take place at least five times a year
- *Home-school connection:* home and school visits for new students; two-way communication notebooks; school-based family group meetings; individual meetings with families; citywide family workshops.

Funding for Expansion and Fidelity

By 2005, the NYCPS was inundated with parental requests for admission of their kindergarten-age students to the ASD Nest program. Parents expected effective educational interventions for their children who received an autism classification. To meet that demand, the NYCPS offered the ASD Nest program to selected additional schools.

At that time, the NYCPS awarded New York University five-year contracts to support the ASD Nest program and its replication at additional school sites. Similarly, the NYCPS awarded Hunter College five-year contracts to provide training, developed by Shirley, for new Nest staff. This training and support model continued for years. As of 2021, funding for both program support and training was provided exclusively to New York University.

Each ASD Nest program opened with one or two kindergarten classes and added one higher grade level each year. By 2011, the nineteen elementary schools that were sites for the ASD Nest program had 121 ASD Nest classes in kindergarten through fifth grade, with about 450 autistic students being educated in those classes alongside their typically developing peers.

The selection of new school sites is a centralized function within the NYCPS, now housed in the Office of Specialized Programs. The first criterion for an ASD Nest school site is whether there is a need for the program in a particular community. In the early years, the decision to open a Nest program was often influenced by the staunch advocacy of families in some districts. Over time, however, as a matter of equity, the NYCPS began to use data to drive decision-making about opening new ASD Nest sites. In any community school district not currently served by the program, site selections are made based on the number of five-year-olds classified as autistic for whom the Nest program is the appropriate placement.

The next criterion for school sites is the availability of sufficient space in a school to house the program. NYCPS teams assess the spatial capacity of potential school sites. Space is a precious commodity in NYC, and many schools are overcrowded. In the first few years, the model typically had two ASD Nest classes per grade from kindergarten through fifth grade, which required schools to be able to provide up to twelve additional classrooms for a fully implemented program, in addition to space for speech/language and occupational therapists. In later years, in part for this reason, some new Nest programs were launched with only one Nest class per grade.

A final selection criterion is how well a school functions. NYCPS examines questions such as: Is the principal a strong instructional leader and a knowledgeable supporter of inclusion? Does the school reflect a positive attitude toward disabled students and those with complex support needs? Is the school meeting academic standards?

Once a site is selected, the NYU Nest Support Team and NYCPS conduct a comprehensive onboarding process. Through this process, the model is explained, the benefits of having an ASD Nest program are showcased, and the school principal's concerns and hopes are addressed in order to implement the ASD Nest program in a manner that enhances the school culture and community. In addition, principals often have already heard from their colleagues that the ASD Nest program enriches the whole school through its strategies and resources. As one principal wrote:

CHAPTER 1

> The ASD Nest program has made me a better principal. In addition to providing a quality education for children on the autism spectrum, the ASD Nest structure has improved the education of all students in my school. The best analogy I can give is this: The Nest program has acted like a big rock that is tossed into a pond. The excellent structures and strategies learned in this program have spread out to include the entire school community. From the team meeting structure to the language and strategies of the Nest, we are a better school because of the ASD Nest program!
>
> *(D. Troy-Quinn, personal communication, November 2008)*

Replication of the ASD Nest program requires a commitment to implementing the core features of the model. A large body of research shows the critical importance of fidelity of implementation (O'Donnell 2008). Therefore, beyond the onboarding process, the NYCPS and NYU Support Project are committed to providing ongoing support, training, and partnership with all ASD Nest program schools and their staff. Fidelity to core components of the ASD Nest program has been sufficiently demonstrated at almost all sites. That commitment and meticulous attention to fidelity of implementation is one of the most important drivers of Nest's success.

Another necessary driver of success is NYCPS's consistent provision of the funding each school needs to successfully implement the program with fidelity. This includes an additional allocation to each school for reduced class size, Integrated Co-teaching structures and staffing, staffing to support parent engagement, and staff to participate in team meetings and Nest professional development activities.

In 2013, Brenda Smith Myles, PhD, an international speaker, consultant, and author on autism, wrote the following in the Preface of the original ASD Nest book:

- This ASD Nest Model works.
- It is a model that can and should be replicated.
- The ASD Nest Model has and will continue to change long-term outcomes.

As of fall 2023, the ASD Nest Model had been replicated in eighty-three elementary, middle, and high school sites. The solidity and consistency of the NYU and NYCPS collaboration is a major reason for the Nest program's success for over twenty years.

CHAPTER 2

The Nest Student

Dorothy Siegel and Shirley Cohen

Who is this child, the typical Nest student?
Answer: There is no "typical" ASD Nest student.

The ASD Nest program serves students starting in kindergarten who meet the criteria for the educational classification of autism. In New York State, toddlers can qualify for services through New York State's Early Intervention Program for children with developmental delays or conditions closely associated with such delays; then from ages three to five, children can qualify as "a disabled preschool child" through a state-approved preschool special education program. In New York, any preschool-age child who fits the state educational category of autism is eligible for preschool special education services. Therefore, many students entering the ASD Nest program have received intervention services for one or more years, while others have not previously received any special education services.

Each student in the Nest program is unique. A Nest student's areas of strengths, challenges, and interests can vary widely, as they would for any student. None of these factors preclude a student from being placed in Nest. The NYCPS's process for placement of students into the Nest program is designed to ensure that students are placed appropriately into a program that meets their needs in the most inclusive setting in community schools, learning alongside students with and without Individualized Education Programs (IEP).

To be successful in the ASD Nest program, children must be able to master the academic curriculum and standards of the grade they are in. In the NYC public schools, even at the kindergarten level—which is when most children are admitted to the ASD Nest program—children are expected to master certain skills in reading, writing, and mathematics when provided the appropriate supports. ASD Nest class sizes are reduced, and there are only four students with IEPs and up to eight students without IEPs in kindergarten, which increases to sixteen children in first grade and twenty children in fourth grade.

Supports in the Nest program are class wide and student specific, especially as academic content becomes increasingly abstract and the expectation for independent and group work intensifies. The Nest program also provides support in sensory processing and social communication, areas that often interfere with student learning and success.

Although most students enter the Nest program in kindergarten, some start Nest at an older age and grade. Reasons for students joining the Nest program after kindergarten can vary. Some students are classified with autism at a later age, while other students start out in a non-Nest classroom but struggle as the academic and social demands change as students move into upper grades. Often, for entrance after kindergarten, struggling non-Nest students are identified mid-year as being appropriate for, and better served in, the Nest program. In those cases, they may be added to a Nest class at that time or the following fall, with transition supports to ease their entry.

The first step of the admission process for kindergarten-age children is the dissemination of information about the ASD Nest program. This is arguably the most important step, as the NYCPS's goal is to identify and place autistic students from all demographics and geographic backgrounds entering the NYC public school system into the appropriate settings. New York City Public Schools (NYCPS) disseminates information to preschool programs, information and referral centers, and parent advocacy agencies. Moreover, between November and March, NYCPS holds informational meetings in each borough for parents of preschoolers with disabilities. One of the programs described at these meetings is the ASD Nest program. Most importantly, NYCPS has strengthened awareness of the Nest program through the IEP process, encouraging school psychologists and social workers to discuss this program with parents and caregivers as they go through the IEP process, either initially or at the annual review.

Families interested in having their child considered for the ASD Nest kindergarten complete and submit an ASD application form. The admission process has changed during the past ten years to further promote easy and equitable access. The Central Autism Team in the NYCPS Special Education Office reviews applications in collaboration with the school-based support teams responsible for creating the Individualized

Education Program. The application form, available through the NYCPS public website, requires families to complete the form with only their child's basic information and indicate a desire for a child to be placed in the Nest program. More assessment data is collected after NYCPS reviews the candidate's application. A complete package for a child who has been receiving intervention services typically includes a recent psychological evaluation and social history, educational progress reports, speech-language and other related service progress reports, and any medical or other outside evaluations. It is important to note that students who can be supported in the Nest program do not need to have a medical diagnosis of autism to be admitted to the program. All Nest students must be found eligible for an educational classification of autism. These evaluations and assessments can all be done, free of charge, through NYCPS's Individualized Education Program process. The application review process includes the student's prior testing, prior special education assessment, teacher and related service providers' progress notes, previous IEPs, and consultation with the student's family and current school team. After the clinical review of assessment materials and an initial determination that a student can be supported in the Nest program, an observation is conducted in the student's current educational setting. The purpose of the observation is to confirm the student's skill levels as reported in the clinical record, to observe the current supports in the non-Nest setting, and to match program supports to a student's learning needs.

NYCPS Eligibility Criteria for Student Placement in the ASD Nest program:

- Eligible for an educational disability classification of autism.
- Average to above-average intelligence with consistent development, including verbal and nonverbal abilities, working memory, language, and attention.
- Academic skills on or above grade level
    - Students are able to work independently and in small groups with minimal support.
    - Students participate in standard assessments, including New York State (NYS) Math and English Language Arts (ELA) exams.
- Accommodations are provided as written on the student's IEP.
- Language skills on or close to age level, except in social language.
- Mild to moderate social delays. May demonstrate challenges in interacting and/or playing with peers or adults.

- Behavior challenges related to autism. May demonstrate challenging behavior related to their experience (e.g., elopement to get away from overwhelming sensory environment or to find connection with a preferred staff member).
- May demonstrate challenges with:
  - Handling changes in routine.
  - Monitoring and regulating their own emotions and behaviors.

Let's meet four preschool children at the time they were being considered for admission to the Nest program. All of them were admitted to ASD Nest kindergarten classes and subsequently flourished there.

The names of students in this book and some small details have been changed to protect privacy, and some of the scenarios are amalgamations for the purpose of illustration.

Jorge

Jorge presents as an enthusiastic youngster who attends a special education preschool. He rarely interacts with other students and prefers solitary activity. Jorge frequently engages in hand stimming (the repetitive performance of certain physical movements) and pacing across the day. He continually verbally communicates to his teachers, service providers, and even visitors what he is doing at a given moment: "Now I am eating snack," or, "I put the ball on the table." He interacts with his peers only when directed to do so by his teacher. Jorge appears to have some language-processing issues. His nonverbal IQ score is much higher than his verbal score, and while he has above-average expressive language skills, his receptive language skills are below average. Jorge becomes easily overstimulated and has a great deal of difficulty with self-regulation.

Alia

Alia attends a general education preschool program with support from a special education itinerant teacher for fifteen hours a week. Alia's preschool encourages child-centered activities and allows a lot of time for free choice. Thus, Alia could engage in a play activity for a long period of time. However, she often stays with an activity for only a few minutes before moving to another one, and at times she wanders around the room. Although Alia seeks out other children to play with, they reject her overtures because she has difficulty navigating the social environment, resulting in confrontations with other children. In addition, her behavior is developmentally immature and surprising at times. For example, she pretends to be a dog by walking around on all fours and barking while the other children play with blocks and talk to each other.

Abdul

Abdul has an intense interest: subway maps and train lines. Every time he meets someone, he asks that person where they live and then proceeds to tell them which train to take to get to their home or school. Abdul attends a general education preschool. At first when observing him, it is hard to pinpoint areas of challenge. He is attentive to the teacher's instructions and responds readily to questions. However, his peer interactions are quite limited. He often appears eager to engage with others around him but can't sustain the interaction. He may start a conversation with, "Hi ______ (name of person)," but has difficulty continuing the conversation after that. He is responsive to questions but does not initiate communication except about his specific interests (i.e., subway maps and train lines). Abdul has developmentally appropriate cognitive abilities as well as academic skills.

Chris

Chris attends a neighborhood preschool program with full-time support from a one-to-one aide. His program follows a daily schedule with predictable centers. He easily engages in the centers; his favorite is the sensory station with sand, water, or beads to use and manipulate. He seems to enjoy engaging with peers, and they with him. However, if his peers change how the collaborative activity is being played, he screams or throws a toy. Chris has strong receptive language and uses echolalic expressive language, repeating dialogue from favorite movies or repeating words back to others when they ask him questions. He has limited spontaneous verbal language.

The ASD Nest program is a great program for many children with ASD, but not for all such children. However, many children who present significant behavioral or language challenges in their preschool settings may flourish in the positive and supportive ASD Nest environment. Leon was such a child.

Leon

The school year had started two weeks earlier, and Leon still did not have an educational program placement. He was of the appropriate age to enter kindergarten and had received both early intervention and preschool special education services. He had been given a diagnosis of PDD-NOS (Pervasive Developmental Disorder—Not Otherwise Specified) before age three, appeared to have limited communication skills, interacted very little with his same-age peers in the preschool special education program he had attended, and appeared to have no pre-academic skills. The school psychologist could not complete a cognitive assessment that she considered valid because Leon cried throughout that evaluation session and wandered off several times.

There was an opening in one of the ASD Nest kindergartens in his zoned school, and since no other appropriate program had been identified for Leon, he was admitted. At first his teachers were concerned. Leon wouldn't join in any group activities, wandered around the room, and cried almost all through the school day. The consultant (Shirley Cohen) told the team that although she wasn't sure that this was the right program for Leon, he was there, and they had to do their best to design a useful plan for him.

With Shirley's help, such a plan was developed. It focused on creating a parallel curriculum delivered on a one-to-one basis plus very short periods of group participation during activities in which Leon showed some interest. Thus, when the class was learning to write letters of the alphabet at the front of the room with one teacher, the other teacher worked with Leon at a table at the back of the room with the letters of his first name that she had drawn in two dimensions and had Leon color in with crayons. (Leon liked to use crayons.) When the class was singing a good morning song, the teacher who was not leading the group brought Leon to the carpet where the children were sitting and sat with him for the length of the song. (Leon liked music.) Then they returned to coloring at the table in the back of the room. When one of the teachers was instructing the class on reading numbers, the other teacher brought Leon into the group for a few minutes and helped him participate. (Leon seemed interested in numbers.)

One day while coloring, Leon amazed his teacher by naming all the colors in a crayon box that contained five or six colors. He also began participating in group math instruction, showing that he could recognize and name numbers, and began participating in singing the good morning song. Leon, who was given a seat at a table next to a peer mentor, began trying to copy the table work the peer mentor was doing, with her assistance from time to time.

By late winter, a decision had to be made about next year's placement. While Leon did not meet most kindergarten standards, he was making so much progress that the team decided to give him a chance at first grade, and that spring Leon began making major strides.

Let's take a peek at Leon in the fifth grade. He is doing grade-level work, loves school, and demonstrates meaningful social communication. His father told the ASD Nest team that he had had no hope for his son's future until Leon was promoted to first grade in the ASD Nest program. Then he knew his son would "make it." And Leon is "making it."

Leon is now a high school graduate with a job he loves whose family is very proud of him and his growing self-advocacy skills.

CHAPTER 2

Because some children like Leon know more than they can show when being evaluated for entry into the Nest program, admission criteria are used as a guide rather than as a rigid set of rules.

CHAPTER 3

The Nest Classroom

Shirley Cohen and Brandy Stanfill-Hobbs

A Visit to a Nest Classroom

Upon walking into a Nest kindergarten classroom one spring morning, the first words that came to my mind were "organized" and "calming." Bulletin boards were covered in light blue, and every item in the room had its place. Bins were color-coded and labeled. Moving closer to the meeting area, I saw that the morning activities were listed so the students could follow along. Off to the side were the student tables, each with seating for four, and each with its own name. Some student table spaces had reminder cards on them, one with a checklist for arrival, including unpacking steps with a picture of the student executing the steps successfully.

With the sound of a soft bell and a cue from the teachers gesturing toward the carpet, the students moved to the meeting area, chanting, "Time for morning meeting." One student went to the break area to carry out his scheduled movement activities with help from one of the teachers prior to joining the group on the carpet. Another student then gestured to that teacher to sit next to her, and the teacher did that, recognizing this child's need for support. The morning meeting opened with both teachers welcoming the class, "I am so happy to see everyone of class K-123 here today."

The classroom is the hub of the ASD Nest program. It is here that most of the "action" takes place and children learn, play, and grow with non-autistic peers in a community school. The major tools for helping make the program succeed in this mission in its early years were "Guideposts for Staff of the ASD Nest program" (Cohen and Bleiweiss 2007); "Expanded Classroom Guideposts for the ASD Nest program" (Bleiweiss et al. 2011); and its companion, "The Three-Tier Model of Supports for the Nest program" (Hough et al. 2011). The forerunners of these guides were presented in chapter I. The Nest program now uses the Elementary Guide, which is explored in chapter 10.

The premise of the Guideposts is that school-based interventions can help many autistic children learn to function more effectively both in school and outside of school, leading to better school experiences, fuller childhoods, and more promising long-term developmental trajectories. But before an elementary school joins the ASD Nest program, there is much preparation to do. Once the composition of students in each kindergarten class has been established—four children on the autism spectrum and eight children without signs of special education needs—the staff of teachers and related service providers who will work in the program are selected and trained. Additionally, before the school year begins, visits are made to each family home, and each child visits the school and classroom with a family member. (See chapter 6, "Collaborative Structures," for more about these supports.)

Emergence of the Classroom Guideposts

The ASD Nest program expands as new schools are added and already participating schools add another grade level. Few teachers are well prepared to work with autistic children prior to being selected for the program, and the same is true of the speech therapists and occupational therapists who are essential to the program. We recognized that we could not subject autistic children to a long period with teachers and related service providers who had limited understanding of the students' needs and how to support them in a school setting. We knew that we needed to provide guidance and support to incoming staff right from the start. That's why new staff took one or two graduate courses focused on autism in the summer before the start of the school year, with tuition for those courses at Hunter College being offered at no cost to staff through grants from NYC Public Schools. We also realized that staff would need ongoing support when working with their actual Nest class. The creation of two key documents for Nest staff, "Expanded Classroom Guideposts" and "The Three-Tier Model of Strategies and Supports," were a response to that need.

The strategies included in the original "Classroom Guideposts" focused on areas of difficulty common in children with ASD: sensory functioning, social communication and relatedness, self-regulation, and select cognitive processes. Both evidence-based practices and highly promising practices were included in the "Classroom Guideposts," selected to reflect a coherent intervention framework that can be implemented systematically. Training experiences, both pre and in service, and ongoing school-based consultation were used to help ensure an effective implementation process. **Establishing Nest class supports is a process of engaging with new strategies for teachers, therapists, and administrators.**

Let's take a closer look at the why and when of the "Classroom Guideposts." By 2005, an observer entering a Nest kindergarten or first-grade classroom would very likely note that it differed in appearance from most mainstream classes at the same grade level. If the observer stayed for more than a few minutes, they would see differences in how the class functioned. Not only were the Cornerstones of the Nest program (fig. 1.1 in chapter 1) being pursued, but the strategies supporting the achievement of those Cornerstones were also being implemented.

Prevention

> *There is now compelling evidence that preventive interventions to support pro-social behavior are most effective in reducing behavior problems in schools (McIntosh et al. 2012, 17).*

The original ASD Nest Model placed a heavy emphasis on strategies designed to prevent the occurrence of behavior that impedes learning or has a disruptive effect on the autistic child and classmates. Many aspects of a mainstream classroom create situations that may overwhelm the coping capacities of autistic learners, and thus set up such a child for a meltdown or other impeding behavior. A teacher's loud voice or negative comments, instructions that are too complex for the student to follow, unexpected changes in the class schedule or other routines, teacher expectations for rapid responses to questions, and lessons that require students to sit on a floor with little movement for long periods of time may all serve as precipitants or triggers for impeding behavior. Prevention strategies were aimed at minimizing such factors.

The Three-Tier Model of Strategies and Supports

"The Classroom Guideposts" provided specific strategies for Nest teams to proactively implement for the whole class. In this chapter, there are a sample of those strategies that can and have been implemented within the Nest framework, but in addition to presenting strategies, the model had to address differences in the intensity of interventions needed by individual students. A tiered system of Nest supports was created for that purpose.

"The Three-Tier Model" served as an organizational framework for the interventions used in the Nest program. The needs of autistic students vary greatly across academic, social, sensory, and behavior domains, so a tiered system of supports made good sense. All Tier 1 strategies and several listed in Part ll support prevention.

Tier I

Tier I consisted of strategies and supports that were designed for use with all students, included teaching practices that were reflective of current research, and were consistent with high-quality core instruction (VanDerheyden and Burns 2010.) Many of the Tier I strategies and supports were designed to be implemented at the whole-class level and can benefit typically developing children as well as autistic learners. Most Tier I practices can be conceptualized as preventive practices. Examples include the following:

- Frequent opportunities for student choice making
- Positive reinforcement of student behavior
- Balancing of calming and arousing activities
- Incorporating movement activities into the daily schedule
- Displaying task boards that list the sequential steps in completing tasks
- Incorporating student interests into class activities

Tier II

Tier II addressed the needs of students for whom Tier I supports were not sufficient. Tier II consisted of more individualized supports, which were delivered in a one-to-one format initially and could later be implemented in a dyad or a group with three or four children.

Movement to Tier II required a team review to ascertain that Tier I strategies had been implemented as designed and that a particular student needed the additional interventions in Tier II. Examples of Tier II interventions include the following:

- Priming
- Social narratives

- Role playing
- Individualized movement activities
- Help cards and break cards
- Headphones
- Peer mentoring
- Individual "office" (study carrel)
- Extra processing time for responding to questions
- Simplifying assigned tasks by breaking them into smaller segments

Several Tier II strategies are presented later in this chapter.

Tier III

Tier III provided highly targeted intervention for students who experienced intensive or extensive challenges and needed interventions beyond those in Tiers I and II. Tier III required multicomponent interventions created in conjunction with an instructional consultant from NYU or Hunter College. These interventions required close monitoring with ongoing data collection and team reviews. Movement to Tier III intervention was often preceded by a meeting with the student's family.

Examples of Tier III interventions:

- Create an individual positive reinforcement system with ongoing monitoring
- Simplify tasks that are challenging for the student
- Provide one-to-one priming on all new learning material
- Schedule a short sensory break during every sedentary work period or between two such periods
- Re-teach use of a help card and a break card as appropriate

Positive and Proactive Support

The positive behavior support paradigm used in the Nest program during its foundational years was a process of preventing, teaching, and reinforcing (Dunlap et al. 2010). Positive behavior supports were used to prevent behavior that interfered with learning, to respond to such behavior helpfully when it occurred, and to develop replacement skills and behaviors.

At one school, a teacher who had experience at the kindergarten level kept a large chart at the front of her Nest classroom to which she added names of students who had not followed her directives to her satisfaction. That chart was clearly not a positive response, as even her five-year-old students recognized. So, too, did her co-teacher, who reminded her that a central ASD Nest consultant was coming to observe the program that afternoon. By the time the consultant arrived, the chart had been totally redone. Now it described what each student had done well.

That teacher came to recognize the power of positive reinforcement and, over time, became outstanding in her work within the ASD Nest program to the benefit of all her students (Cohen and Hough 2013).

Establishing a Supportive Learning Environment

Nest classrooms are designed to be supportive and engaging learning spaces. Care is taken to avoid sensory overload and to provide opportunities for regulation. Well-organized, sensory-neutral learning spaces can set autistic learners up for academic and social engagement. *Students with autism learn and connect best when they feel safe and physically comfortable.* Without support, they are likely to experience greater challenges in maintaining a state of regulation for extended periods of time than their typically developing peers. Therefore, the Nest classroom was designed as a therapeutic space.

What's Different? Visitors to Nest classrooms often notice that bookcases are covered with cloth when not in use and that the walls have fewer decorations than in other classrooms. They may note that some of the overhead lights are dimmed or off and that the only charts or slides displayed are for the current lesson. Visitors often comment on the subdued colors covering the bulletin boards and the clear labels on cabinets, baskets, student supplies, and the break area.

Even in classrooms designed to reduce stimulation, break areas draw attention and curiosity from visitors. Break areas are small, offset, areas in the classroom which may include bean bag chairs, pillows, or mats so that students can sit or lie comfortably and are stocked with tools that support self-regulation, like fidgets, noise-canceling headphones, and books (see chapter 8 for more information on break areas). "How do they work?" is a common question. While Nest classrooms vary by grade, or in the case of departmentalized upper elementary grades, by subject or focus, the essentials of the break area are the same across the program. Break areas are accessible to all students in the classroom, not just autistic students. Students who are feeling overwhelmed may ask to go to the break area, or the option to go to the break area may be offered by a teacher or therapist. Once in the break area, a student might choose to manipulate fidgets, use a headphone, read or page through a book, or do simple stretching exercises taught by the occupational therapist who works with that child and class. Students who have an established break routine may set a timer based on the amount of time they usually need to calm themselves and self-regulate. When the timer goes off, students return to the group, and teachers support them in re-engaging with their work as needed.

"And why are the bookcases covered? Why aren't there charts hanging all around the room? Why are the lights dimmed?" visitors often inquire. The answer to each of those questions is the same: well-organized, sensory-neutral learning spaces can set autistic learners up for academic and social engagement. Taking the visual perspective of an autistic student seated on the classroom rug for a lesson in a non-Nest class, it quickly becomes clear that there are many things to distract a child. There are rows, stacks, and baskets of books; colorful labels; books on stands across the top of bookcases; stuffed animals and decorations scattered around the classroom library; a board or easel; a teacher chair, often with its own colorful label; and charts hanging above the bookcases. There is a riot of color and letters and shapes and textures for children to attend to that may compete with lessons. In a Nest classroom, a host of distractions are eliminated, and the likelihood that a child will be able to attend to and make meaning from the lesson is increased.

A Sensory Challenge: Sounds That Hurt

One of the schools in the Nest pilot had a large kindergarten room that included a built-in area for toileting and handwashing. The teachers modeled flushing the toilet and washing hands before returning to the main classroom. Each child was then given a chance to demonstrate how to do that. One student covered his ears and refused to participate. When the teacher repeated the process with that child individually, he screamed as the teacher flushed the toilet. The teacher noted that this toilet made a particularly loud sound when it was flushed. After discussing the child's response at a team meeting, a set of sound-muffling headphones was placed inside the toileting area, and the teacher showed the student how to put the headphones on before flushing the toilet. This use of headphones worked well not only for this child and for toileting but also in other unavoidable situations involving certain loud sounds like those made during the school's practice fire drills.

This anecdote illustrates how a challenging situation in a Nest class led to team problem-solving and the identification of an appropriate strategy for responding to that challenge. Other examples of this process of matching strategies to needs follow.

Modulating Voice Levels

Teacher or therapist voice volume and rate of speech can be significant contributing factors to student overstimulation that impacts learning and engagement. Speaking at a reduced volume and pace and allowing adequate processing time can reduce cognitive load for autistic learners.

A necessary first ingredient for achieving this is the modeling of appropriate voice levels by teachers and other program staff. Because educators speak at a pace and volume that feels comfortable to them, it's easy to overlook or misinterpret the impact of volume and rate of speech on autistic students. Nest teachers are careful to observe student reactions to their voice volume, including signs of discomfort like students turning away, covering their ears, increasing their own voice levels, or increasing their intensity of stimming. It's helpful to keep in mind that some students may not show signs of discomfort but may become more engaged when addressed at a volume they find comfortable.

Student voice volume can be another easily overlooked source of sensory overload, and five-point voice scales are used in Nest to teach all students the voice levels to use for various class and school activities. If you enter a Nest classroom, you are very likely to notice a scale like the one below on display. The scale may also be used to label and explain the intensity of feelings or the "size" of a problem, etc.

FIGURE 3.1. Voice Scale from PS 682, based on the Incredible 5-Point Scale, Buron and Curtis 2012

The Incredible 5-Point Scale and Andrew

Andrew was five years old, but he was a big child with a very big voice that was often heard in the hallway and in the classrooms next door. The Incredible 5-Point Scale was taught to the class with modeling by the teacher and games with the students, who were asked questions about what voice levels the teachers were using, and were also asked to use different voice levels themselves during selected activities. Still, Andrew's voice boomed out as if he was calling to someone at the other end of the large schoolyard. At that point, a miniature version of the 5-Point Scale was created for Andrew. He kept it on his table in the classroom, put it in his pocket when he left the room, and took it home each day to show his mother how he used it. After several weeks, Andrew more easily recognized the differences in voice levels and more frequently used a voice level appropriate for each school activity engaged in by his class.

The Classroom "Office"

Michael was in a second-grade Nest class. He found it hard to focus on work when students were moving about the room or passing his seat. He was distracted when students sitting close to him conferred with each other, even when they spoke in a level 2 whisper. After his teachers discussed this situation with their Nest team, they created an "office" on one side of the classroom. The "office" was actually a study carrel consisting of a desk and chair surrounded at the front and sides by dividers to block out the view of the classroom and lower the sound level. A sign announced that this was "Michael's Office." Other students gathered around and asked questions about it. The teacher explained that it helped Michael concentrate on his work. Other students were curious and wanted to know if they could use the office, so the teachers set up a routine that allowed Michael's classmates to use the "office" when Michael didn't need it.

Priming for Change

Coping with changes is often challenging for autistic children. This is particularly true when the change is unexpected.

Each morning Adam's father walked him the five blocks from their home to his school. They took the same route every day, until several weeks into the school year when Adam's father made a different turn. When Adam recognized that this was not the route he was accustomed to, he became very upset, screaming and pulling at his father to "go the right way." Eventually, they reached the school, but Adam remained highly anxious for the rest of the day, and his father was distraught. What should be done? was the question discussed at the team meeting later that week. Adam's parents had tried to avoid distress and overstimulation by sticking to routines as closely as possible, but now that Adam was five years old and in school, they were becoming quite concerned. A plan was developed to help Adam by preparing him for changes before they were made using priming.

Priming is a powerful tool for supporting students who become anxious or dysregulated by changes or novel experiences, particularly if those changes are unexpected. Priming is essentially preparation for new learning experiences and expectations. It can be done one-to-one, in small groups, or with the whole class under relaxed conditions *before* the new activity or change takes place.

Priming may be as simple as reading a picture book with a kindergartener before it is read to the class and children are expected to answer questions about it. Priming may involve introducing a student to a new math procedure, or making up riddles before a group lesson on that subject. Priming has also been used in the Nest program with whole classes as preparation for new whole-group experiences like spelling bees, field trips, and fire drills.

Social Narratives

Social narratives are an evidence-based strategy designed for autistic learners that uses personalized stories to share information, teach a skill, or identify a situation to a commonly occurring challenge. Social Stories™ are a particular type of social narrative developed (and trademarked) by Carol Gray (2010) that was frequently used during the ASD Nest early years.

Social narratives are used in the ASD Nest program as priming tools, to support student understanding of and access to classroom routines and procedures, and to teach self-care skills. They are also often used to support student regulation and to help students cope with change. Adam and his teacher wrote a Social Story about what happened on the day his father took a different route to Adam's school and Adam became upset. The story closed by stating, "there are different ways to walk to school, and that's OK." On some days Adam chooses the way, and on other days his father chooses the way. A photograph of Adam and his father walking to school together was on the last page. Adam kept his narrative in his book bag after he "read" it to his class.

In another Nest kindergarten, a social narrative took the form of a series of photographs of a student who insisted on being first in line every time the class left the classroom. Verbal explanations alone didn't dent Robert's determination to be first, but when a series of photographs of Robert in different line positions was added, Robert started smiling. Each page of Robert's storybook showed a photo of him in a different position in the line, with one sentence labeling that position, e.g., "Today Robert is second in line." Soon, Robert was changing positions while referring to his place in line in his story book—and continuing to smile.

Video Modeling

Sometimes strategies for coping with change are combined for greater effectiveness, particularly when the change or novelty involved is likely to cause dysregulation for some young students. Video modeling is one strategy that addresses such situations. Video modeling is an evidence-based practice in which you break down situations into steps, record someone acting out those steps, and use the recording to help teach skills and routines or to prime for new situations. Let's look at practice fire drills, in which the loud sound of clanging bells may make young students very anxious. During a fire drill, children are expected to line up quickly and quietly in an orderly manner, but several students in an ASD Nest class became upset. The teachers of that Nest kindergarten class decided that something needed to be done to prevent this from happening each time another fire drill took place. A videotape of the procedure to be followed by students during a fire drill was created, with the students practicing appropriate behavior through role-playing. The videotaped role play was effective in reducing student anxiety, and it motivated other Nest teachers to consider using that strategy too.

Daily Class Schedules

Autistic learners benefit from predictable classroom environments. When routines and procedures are clear and easy to follow, students are better able to process information, make choices, and engage with peers and teachers. Daily class schedules can serve as organizers and reference points. Nest practitioners post and actively reference classroom schedules across the day, often checking off completed activities, or turning or removing cards from a schedule pocket chart. This allows students to easily reference the schedule to see what has been completed and what is next, which supports self-regulation. Schedules should be located for easy reference by students and be large enough to see easily from any area of the room.

Once students are accustomed to the class schedule and feel safe and connected with teachers and peers, Nest teachers may begin introducing change into the schedule. After students have been primed for a change, teachers can insert a surprise activity into the daily schedule about once a week on different days and times. Initially, the surprise should be something that's novel, fun, or exciting; later in the school year some of the surprises can be neutral. Starting with surprises that students are likely to enjoy can help build comfort, reduce stress around change, and teach children that there are multiple ways to respond to change.

Thursday	
Period 1	Reading
Period 2	Independent Reading
Period 3	?
Period 4	Lunch & Recess
Period 5	Writing
Period 6	Science Centers
Period 7	Gym

FIGURE 3.2. Introducing novelty/change in a schedule

Additional Visual Supports

Many autistic learners process visual information more efficiently than auditory input and benefit from the support of visual aids to better understand learning tasks. Used in tandem with, or in some cases in place of verbal instruction, visuals can clarify tasks and procedures and support engagement with partners or small groups, thus contributing significantly to the well-being of autistic students (Hodgdon 1995). However, visual aids must be used with care. A Nest classroom overrun with charts and other visual stimuli can create a confusing maze for a young learner.

Procedure charts can be powerful tools for supporting students in carrying out both new and recurring classroom tasks. Nest elementary classrooms commonly use procedure charts to support packing and unpacking at the beginning and end of the school day, lining up for recess or other activities, getting out or putting away classroom materials, or engaging in partner discussion during lessons. Each procedure is actively taught and regularly reviewed, and the chart is posted when students will benefit from referencing it. Charts and other visuals are put away when not in use to reduce the possibility of distraction or overstimulation.

Labels are also used in Nest classrooms to help students find needed materials and return them to the appropriate location after use. For example, a classroom unpacking chart may include the step, "Put your homework folder in the homework bin," and the bin is labeled with a large and easy-to-read "Homework Bin" label or a familiar icon, especially in early grades.

Task analysis, the process of breaking an activity down into its component steps to make the process more manageable and accessible, is frequently used to support autistic learners. For example, in a typical classroom, a teacher may give the instructions to "unpack," which may be too vague for autistic students to implement. So, in a Nest classroom, a standard of practice is to create an "unpacking chart" for the whole class using a task analysis to break down the process. Since students enter at varying levels, an individual may need the "unpacking chart" broken down into smaller steps, especially if they enter after the school year has begun and miss the associated practice the other students already received. Where the class chart says, "Hang up your coat," the new student's task analysis might be more detailed (see chart below). The student using this tool might check off each step with a crayon or marker, or the steps might be laminated and attached to a clipboard with Velcro so each step may be removed and set aside as it's completed.

Unpacking Chart
❑ Take off your coat, mittens, and hat
❑ Hang your coat on the hook under your name
❑ Put your hat and mittens in the cubby above your coat hook

FIGURE 3.3. Task analysis for unpacking

Opportunities for Making Choices

Choices are especially important for autistic learners as choice making can support engagement and learning. However, making choices may be stressful for some children and may take longer or require more support for an autistic student than a non-autistic student. Classrooms offer abundant opportunities for supportive choice making with students who struggle. Methods for supportive choice making include offering a limited number of options—research suggests that three is an ideal number (Iyengar and Lepper 2000), or providing visual support for the options, which can be a list, images of the choices, or the tasks laid out on a surface. Additionally, students should have a non-verbal way to indicate their choice—pointing, checking off or circling the choice on a list, or removing Velcroed images from a choice board. Whenever possible, choices should include options that align with the student's areas of interest and allow them to utilize their strengths. For example, for a student who is interested in amphibians and for whom memorizing facts and details is a strength, you might create an amphibian book bin to select from during independent reading, offer the student guidance in creating a facts book to share with the class, or give the student an option to write and draw images about cold-blooded animals for their project.

How do you want to work?		
Independently	With a partner	With my table group

FIGURE 3.4. Choice board for options of how to engage in work

In the ASD Nest Model, RECOGNIZING THE POWER OF POSITIVE AND PROACTIVE SUPPORT IS CENTRAL TO SUCCESFUL OUTCOMES.

Moving Toward More Neurodiversity-Affirming Practices

As the Nest program evolved, it moved toward more neurodiversity-affirming practices. Nest practitioners work to address behavior in a holistic manner that takes into account the individual neurotype of each child. The strategies in use in Nest classrooms are designed to help practitioners think outside the bounds of a specific behavioral challenge and consider the function of any challenging behavior. How do the perspectives of each person involved in the situation play a part in the challenge? What kinds of things can be done on a whole-class level so that our class environments are meeting all the needs—including the behavioral needs—of our students? In the Nest Model, there is a specific focus on adaptive problem-solving and self-advocating. Thus, the contribution of the students to the culture and norms of the Nest classroom is vital in creating a space where students feel they belong and where students and teachers can work collaboratively when challenges inevitably arrive. Strategies include using supportive and concrete language, providing multiple whole-class and individual opportunities for regulation, and activating students' strengths. These strategies help to avoid confusion, support engagement, and set students up for successful navigation of their day.

Transitions

Transitions are periods of change. As Nest classes moved up to the fifth grade, staff recognized that the ASD Nest Model would need to be modified to fit middle school practices as well as the changing development of the Nest students. By 2010, the Nest program was in place at over a dozen middle schools, and it became clear that a number of modifications of the typical school program would be necessary for the Nest program to be successful at that school level. The Nest middle school model was developed to support autistic learners in the more complex social and academic environment of sixth through eighth grades.

Articulation is the process by which students in NYCPS transition from elementary school to middle school. Since autistic learners are likely to find a change of school environment challenging, the Nest program developed a protocol to support and prepare the students and Nest teams at their new school for this change. The Nest articulation process supplements the general application and placement process and is a year-long process, though much of it happens in the spring, closer to the end of the previous school year.

The first component of this process focuses on the Nest students and is intended to build excitement about their new schools, address questions, and alleviate anxiety/worries about this change. Fifth-grade Nest teams spend time highlighting similarities and differences between elementary and middle school and focus on new tasks and skills to prepare for the transition. For example, fifth graders are often taught to use planners and practice recording their homework and long-term assignments so they are better prepared to keep up with work assigned by multiple teachers in middle school. Elementary and middle schools also collaborate in organizing trips for fifth graders to visit what will be their Nest middle school so that students can meet their new Nest team, see the classrooms, and sit in on a class or other activity.

The second component of this process involves the sending and receiving school teams sharing information about the articulating students. Members of the receiving middle school team visit the sending elementary school to learn more about the students' experiences and the structures they are familiar with, as well as the students' strengths, interests, needs, and current level of support. The elementary school teams prepare articulation packets that summarize useful information about each student, including steps that their new teachers and therapists can take to begin building supportive relationships with the student from day one. Autistic self-advocates were also interviewed about their learning and social experiences and contributed guidance.

Voices of Parents

We have described the Nest program model as it was developed and practiced during its first ten years, with glimpses into the evolving model. In this section we show a sample of what others have told us about the program during that time period and about how it has affected them and their children. The voices of parents are powerful reminders that Nest is all about helping individual children and their families. It is also about producing better teachers, school-based therapists, principals, and schools. We have been doing that, these statements tell us, and we are doing more as we continue to learn more and the model evolves further.

The notes and letters that follow have been modified to protect confidentiality, except in those cases where permission was given to use full names. These comments appeared in the original version of the ASD Nest Model (Cohen & Hough 2013.)

June 18, 2009

Dear Chancellor Klein,

It is with great pleasure that I write you today as the parent of a first-grade child blossoming within the autism spectrum disorder Nest program of PS 186Q, the Castlewood School. It is hard to believe that just one year ago, I wrote to you amid the heartbreaking distress of watching this same sweet child regress into her past autistic symptoms, overwhelmed by the unpredictable world around her, immersed in fears, anxieties, and daily stress as she attended kindergarten in the CTT classroom of our neighborhood school. There, despite the presence of well-meaning educators and support staff, her unique presentation and specific special needs were often misinterpreted, overlooked, and, at worst, ignored.

Following a detailed case review, my daughter was graciously invited to attend the outstanding Nest program of PS 186 as a first-grade student ... I strongly believe that as a direct result of her participation in this groundbreaking educational program, my daughter's former progress is restoring. Her positive strides already exceed our expectations. It is no secret that I consider the Nest program to be nothing short of a miracle in our lives. Not only is it enabling my child to achieve life-altering progress, but it is providing the means by which she may work toward her true potential in a predictable environment adapted to her specific special needs.

I thank you and the New York City Department of Education for the opportunities you have provided my daughter through the Nest program. It has given us back our wonderful child, and one day, I am quite certain, we will be giving it great credit for presenting her to the world.

With sincere appreciation,

Karen M.

CHAPTER 3

March, 2012

Dear Ms. K,

My wife and I are parents of two autistic sons, the younger of whom entered the Nest program in kindergarten and is now in his third year of the Nest program ... We cannot speak highly enough of the Nest program at PS 165Q ... From our first contact, we knew that we had finally found an appropriate placement for E. ... We have been extremely impressed with the intensity and quality of the teachers, therapists, social workers, and most of all the principal, Ms. DeMillio ... Whenever behavioral issues have arisen with E., we have found the school to be highly responsive to our viewpoints and innovative and constructive in creating and implementing successful solutions. E. is flourishing at PS 165Q. He is eager to go to school in the morning and eager to do his homework with us in the afternoon ... We have been particularly struck by Ms. DeMillio's repeated advice that she views the Nest program as the model for the future of her entire school, not simply for the children alone ...

I have no question that the Nest program will become the model system for services at public schools across the country. The genius of the Nest program is that it meets the students halfway. It is the epitome of personalized attention for each student, and the bottom line is that it works ...

Please accept our deepest gratitude for the City's support of the Nest program for our dear son ... We sincerely hope that he can continue to benefit from Nest throughout his public school career.

Thank you and God bless you.

October 25, 2011

When our daughter was diagnosed with Asperger's syndrome a few months earlier, confirming what we had long suspected, [her school] did all they could for us ... She went to a social group once a week and received practical speech therapy. Her teacher ... surpassed her obligations and was a true friend and helper. But it simply was not enough.

There were times when I came to pick her up in the crowded schoolyard, when my daughter was so panicked that she simply froze ... Tantrums were a twice daily occurrence. Increasingly, she shut herself off to me, became more and more depressed, and suffered from mouth ulcers and stomach aches ...

I had heard about the ASD/Nest program at PS 32 ... They told me there wasn't a spot. The waiting list was a mile long. But we got it. We got it!

When my daughter was invited to spend her first visit day at PS 32 ... my husband and I picked her up from the recess yard and got to see something we had never seen before: our daughter running around and playing with other children her age. We stood there for a moment, not wanting to break the spell ... That day was wonderful, and so has every other day been since she started second grade there in September. Since starting PS 32 my daughter has been calm and happy. There have been no tantrums, no depression, no mouth ulcers, and no stomach aches. She constantly talks about how much she lo-o-ves PS 32.[1]

1. Johnson, J. (2011, Oct. 25). Exposed: our neighborhood's hidden gem, the Samuel Mill Sprole School. [Web log comment]. Retrieved from http://carrollgardens.patch.com.

June 17, 2010

Dear Ms. Quinn [principal],

We just wanted to take a moment and say thank you for the wonderful year P. had in K-136 as part of the Nest program. We feel so privileged to have P. in the Nest and PS 186. When we think of how P. is flourishing as a result of your school and the Nest program, we cannot help getting emotional... .

Thank you again for all of your hard work and dedication—it is noticed and appreciated... . I have copied everyone ... because I feel it is important for people to know that their efforts are changing our son's life, and they should be so proud of their accomplishments, as we are.

Sincerely,

P's mom and dad

April 15, 2011

We are the parents of a third grader in the Nest program at PS 206. We are writing to convey to you how important this program is to [him] and his peers ... We thank God that this program exists. There was literally no other option that would have been appropriate for [him]. We shudder to think about what would have happened to [him] if he didn't have the supports that the Nest program provides ...

The DOE has a shining example of the best practices in special education with our Nest program ... one of the few programs that children, parents, teachers, principals and leaders in the field of special education all agree is one of the best that exists for kids.

Sincerely,

M. and D.

August 24, 2010

Hello Ms. Siegel,

With the new school year coming. I had to write to thank you. This fall, my son B. is going into first grade at PS 165 in Queens in the Nest program. Thank you for everything you've done to start and maintain this program. The Nest kindergarten gave B. a great start ... I can't imagine that last year could possibly have been successful without all the elements of Nest ... There was no other setting that was appropriate for his needs. We are so happy that Nest exists.

December 16, 2010

Sheryl Nelson, a mother of a student at PS 19, raves about the DOE's (autism spectrum disorders) Nest program developed by Dorothy Siegel of NYU and Shirley Cohen of Hunter College: "I think they should win the Nobel Prize," Nelson said.[2]

February 16, 2012: [Note from a Nest teacher]

Dear Professor Cohen,

As teachers of the Nest program [at PS 682K], we feel so fortunate to be able to give our students what they need and to be educated [and] supported ...

2. Spielberg, E. Children "On the Spectrum." United Federation of Teachers.

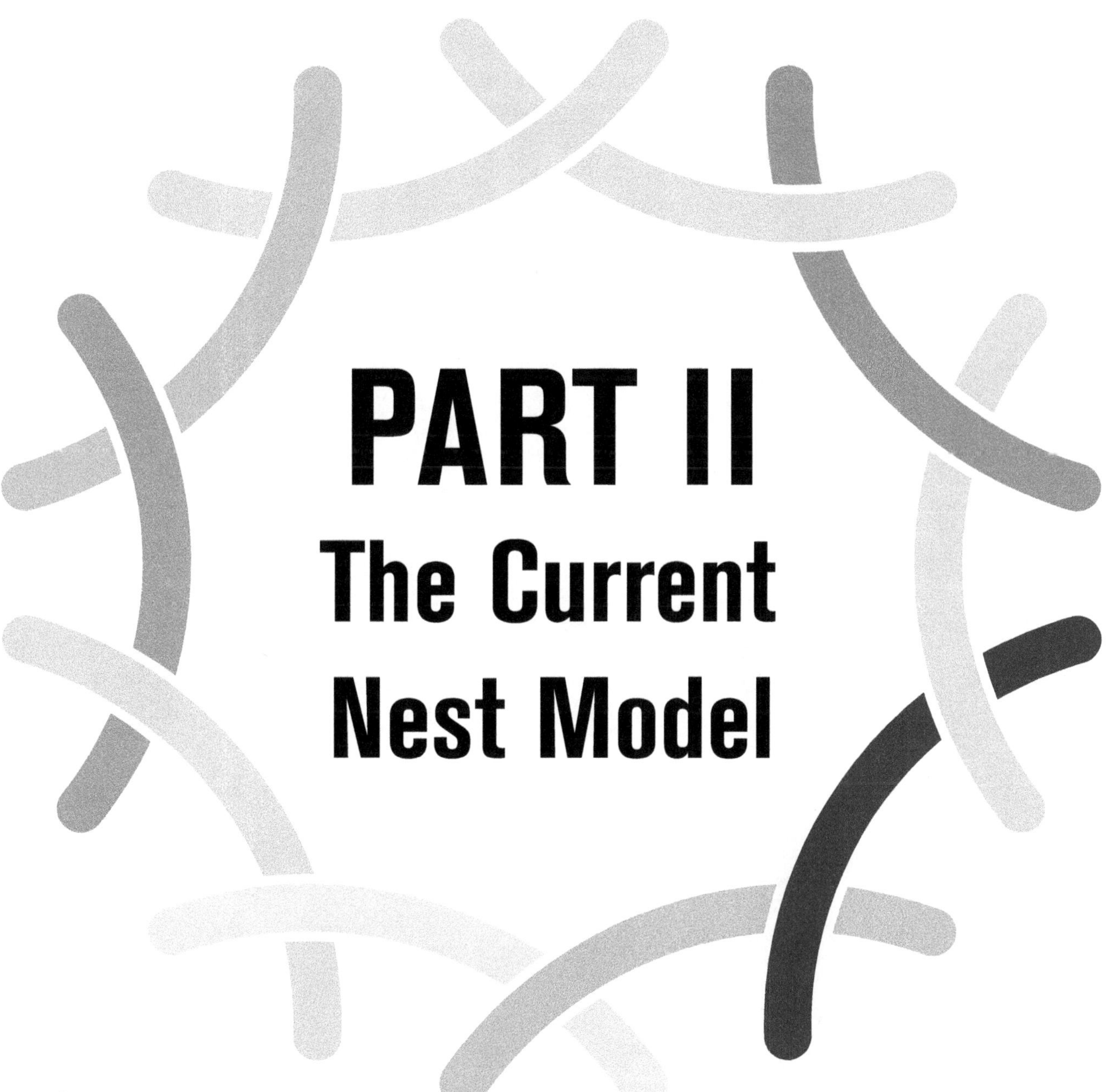

PART II
The Current Nest Model

CHAPTER 4

A Paradigm Shift

Allison Graham Brown

Evolution of the Nest Model

The Nest Model embraces children's inherent neurodiversity, which represents a major paradigm shift in the way we think about children, value them, educate them, and measure their educational success. This is different from the traditional approach to education, in both belief and practice. Traditionally, a student's success is dependent on conforming to school practices in order to meet normative educational and societal standards. The Nest paradigm, on the other hand, centers on the belief that it is not primarily students that need to change, but us, their educators. It is on us to understand that *if students can't learn the way we teach, we must teach them the way they learn* (adapted from Estrada, I. (n.d.)).

Nest is not a stagnant one-size-fits-all model. In the ten years since the first edition of this book was released in 2013, we at the Nest Support Project at NYU have reflected extensively on the model, listened to feedback from key stakeholders, studied the data on Nest program graduates, responded to changes in the field of education, and learned from the autistic advocate community. A lot has happened in society since 2013, especially the COVID-19 pandemic which profoundly impacted the needs of families and students and forced the education system to respond. Society recognized how important it was to focus on social-emotional learning and trauma-informed care as well as academic interventions. The Nest Model adjusted accordingly in order to address these critical areas in ways relevant to Nest students in middle and high school as well as elementary schools.

Partnering with autistic self-advocates drove some of our most important learning during the past decade. In order to ensure that the thinking of autistic individuals informed our work, we collaborated with autistic self-advocates, both as members on our Nest Support Project team and as individual consultants. This diverse group of advocates with whom we worked provided incredible insight from their expertise and intersectional experiences, representative of their multiple overlapping identities, including race, culture, religion, gender expression, sexual identity, and ability, which significantly affected the model's evolution. Their work with Nest included facilitating seminars and workshops for Nest staff and families, participating in learning groups that informed model development, and reviewing Nest resources to ensure that they are responsive to the students we serve.

Over time, our understanding deepened. While staying true to the original foundation and structures, the Nest Model evolved further toward neurodiversity-affirming practices. Nest does not teach autistic students to "fit in," but rather to embrace who they are as individuals so they can reach their personal goals and ultimately achieve a happy and fulfilling life (as they themselves define it!).

Shift in Core Nest Beliefs

One significant element in the evolved model is the centering of anti-ableism in our work. Disability advocate Andrew Pulrang defined ableism as, "Social habits, practices, regulations, laws, and institutions that operate under the assumption that disabled people are inherently less capable overall, less valuable in society, and/or should have less personal autonomy than is ordinarily granted to people of the same age" (Forbes 2020, n.d.). Anti-ableism actively works against that concept. Anti-ableism charges us to interrogate our structures and systems and implores us, as individuals, to consider our language, expectations, and beliefs about disability. In the education field, anti-ableism means recognizing the inherent value of each individual student. Anti-ableism moves us away from standardization, "normality," and rigid definitions of student success so that we may see the value and varied potential of all learners.

In addition to anti-ableism, we also centered the concept of neurodiversity in our thinking. The Nest Model recognizes the factual reality of neurodiversity, a term coined in the late 1990s by journalist Harvey Blume and autism advocate Judy Singer. Neurodiversity, to them, is "the diversity of human minds, the infinite variation in neurocognitive functioning within our species" (Walker 2024). The Nest Model embraces the neurodiversity paradigm, which asserts that all brain types are natural, worthy, and beneficial manifestations of human diversity. This shift in thinking makes true inclusion possible by valuing all learners and fostering consideration of all learners' thoughts and needs in the classroom.

Establishing the Nest program at New Sites

This paradigm shift in Nest strikes many people as running counter to the messages we receive from society and oftentimes our training as educators. For that reason, when expanding the Nest program, it is incumbent on us to deepen key stakeholders' understanding of Nest's philosophical tenets to help them make necessary shifts in their belief system. A paradigm shift in practice can then follow. As Cynthia Coburn has stated, "[Educational] reforms must effect deep and consequential change in classroom practice" (Coburn 2003, 4), which is a result of changes in teachers' beliefs, norms of social interaction, and underlying pedagogical principles. Nest practitioners must have a shared understanding of autism, inclusive education, and other core Nest beliefs. In order to effect the "deep and consequential

Change in Nest Language

The language of Nest also changed over the last decade. We now primarily use identity-first language, which is what many autistic advocates prefer. As advocate Lydia X. Z. Brown stated, "When we say 'Autistic person,' we recognize, affirm, and validate an individual's identity as an Autistic person ... We affirm the individual's potential to grow and mature, to overcome challenges and disability, and to live a meaningful life as an Autistic. Ultimately, we are accepting that the individual is different from non-Autistic people—and recognizing that that's not a tragedy—and we are showing that we are not afraid or ashamed to recognize that difference" (Brown 2011). However, it is up to each individual to decide how they want to be referred to, so expressed personal preferences affect adjustments in language. Additionally, when referencing other groups of people, Nest uses the terms allistic, non-autistic people (including both neurotypicals and non-autistic neurodivergent people), and neurotypical, meaning, "without a defined neurological difference" (Silvertant 2018).

In 2023, our shift in language led us to officially change our name from ASD Nest Support Project to Nest Support Project at NYU. Removing ASD from our name reflects our continuing efforts toward anti-ableism and acknowledges the problematic language associated with the terminology of disorders (the D in ASD). At the same time, in partnership with the NYCPS, the name of the school system's program changed from "ASD Nest program" to "Autism Nest program." We believe that this name change better reflects our values and the model's grounding in the social model of disability (see end of this chapter) and neurodiversity-affirming practices. Parts II and III of this book reflect these changes in language.

change" Coburn calls for, we must first deepen and expand educators' understanding. Further, educators cannot rely solely on Nest guiding documents, as that may result in them giving up when implementation does not go as expected or when challenges arise for situations they encounter which are not addressed in the guiding documents. Therefore, when launching a new Nest program, it is necessary to first develop an understanding of why we approach structures and practices as we do. Once educators make the shift in how they think about their students, a change in their practice will follow more naturally. This deepens practitioners' capacity to do problem-solving rooted in Nest's belief system, and generally leaves them feeling more competent and empowered.

Nest Philosophical Tenets

Nine philosophical tenets, based on the original Nest Model and reflective of its evolution, constitute the foundation of the Nest Model.

AUTHENTIC INCLUSION: Inclusion is not a location; it is a belief that is enacted in all spaces and interactions throughout the school day. It is important that we do not think of Nest as merely an inclusive classroom but rather that inclusion permeates all facets of a Nest school. This includes physical spaces such as hallways, special classes, the cafeteria, and the main office, as well as inclusion opportunities like student clubs, recess, educational programming, field trips, and afterschool programs, in addition to lessons, activities, routines, language, etc. Nest teams ensure that students are authentically included by creating spaces of belonging that convey appreciation for individual uniqueness and identities. Inclusive spaces are those in which students feel seen, heard, valued, and truly welcome. The autistic student is not the sole beneficiary of inclusion: all learners benefit from learning alongside peers with a diversity of experience, perspectives, and strengths.

COLLABORATION: The true expert in any Nest school is the Nest team. The team's collaborative processes facilitate the realization of the Nest program's goals. Nest prioritizes and cultivates partnerships across settings: between members of the school team, alongside families, and with students themselves. Through open and active communication, and guided by the Double Empathy Theory (Milton 2012—see end of chapter), all Nest partners work together to support students in fostering self-determinate lives.

Collaboration is fostered between and across disciplines, within the transdisciplinary team of teachers, related service providers, and school administrators. Collaboration helps team members leverage their unique expertise and experience while actively working together to learn from each other, work together, assess challenges from multiple perspectives, and develop comprehensive and cohesive plans of support. Meaningful collaboration requires a commitment to an ongoing process of communication, partnership, reflection, and collective responsiveness. Thus, the Nest program's goals are realized through an ongoing collaborative process.

UNDERSTANDING AUTISM: Autistic individuals are neurodivergent, meaning they have a different neurotype. In Nest, we affirm that variations in neurological development and functioning across humans are natural and valuable, and we understand that each individual has valuable strengths, perspectives, contributions, and potential. Nest is grounded in the Social Model of Disability (*Fundamental Principles of Disability* 1975), which asserts that people are disabled by barriers in society, not primarily by their impairment or difference. Autistic people are disabled by social and environmental expectations and barriers placed on them by society. Autistic students think and learn differently than allistic (non-autistic) students; accordingly, Nest practices stem from a recognition of students' neurological differences which may manifest as differences in social understanding, sensory sensitivity, self-regulation challenges, etc. However, our goal is not to change our autistic students or to require them to conform to ableist societal expectations; our goal is to enable them to navigate the world in a way that works for them and helps them reach their full and unique potential.

FOCUS ON STRENGTHS: People are more motivated when they do something they're good at—i.e., a strength, and learning is more successful when strengths are engaged/leveraged. Traditional special education focuses on remediating deficit areas. Nest works to develop competency and utilizes strengths to teach and learn. Nest practices are grounded in Self-Determination Theory (Deci and Ryan 1985; see end of chapter), in which competency is one of the three key components of motivation and well-being. That is why, in Nest, students' strengths and interests are honored and meaningfully incorporated into the school day. Engagement in, and deepening of, strengths can lead to empowerment and feelings of fulfillment.

THERAPEUTIC ENVIRONMENT: Nest classrooms are a therapeutic vehicle, designed with students' needs in mind and promoting student well-being. They lead to meaningful engagement and belonging and foster student learning. Nest classrooms are proactively set up in a sensory-safe and organized manner based on what we know about autistic neurology, whereas traditional classrooms are designed to work for "average" students. The Nest therapeutic classroom considers the social, academic, sensory, and regulatory needs of all learners and then intentionally embeds supports into the whole classroom so students can comfortably engage and learn. In a way similar to the Universal Design for Learning (UDL) approach, developed by Dr. David Rose and Dr. Ann Meyer in 1984 at CAST. Nest classrooms create comprehensive accessibility in the physical environment as well as in language, routines, and instructional practices.

SOCIAL DEVELOPMENT: Essential to autistic students' success in school is that their social development is supported by building social cognition and supporting engagement. Nest strives to help students build competence, develop relationships, and address internal motivation, which foster student self-determination and self-advocacy. Nest utilizes a developmental social pragmatic approach known as Social Development Intervention (SDI) scheduled as speech therapy. SDI builds social awareness and differentiated communication tools so that each individual can interact with the world in a way that works best for them. SDI sessions work in tandem with the Nest classroom into which SDI strategies and concepts are woven to promote generalization across contexts. The Nest team considers, plans for, and supports students throughout all social aspects of school, thus facilitating opportunities for autistic learners to meaningfully engage in their whole school environment, have full access to the curriculum, and learn alongside their peers in inclusive settings.

POSITIVE, PROACTIVE SUPPORT: Proactive planning and a pragmatic emphasis on what works leads to meaningful reduction in challenging situations as well as encouragement of new skills. The Nest classroom focuses specifically on adaptive problem-solving and self-advocacy in contrast to compliance. Classroom systems that encourage community and promote a sense of belonging and connection are essentials for both students and educators. Nest staff give attention to potential triggers in the classroom setting and undertake preemptive measures to change the classroom environment, language, structures, and expectations in order to reduce the likelihood of challenges arising and to support self-regulation. Staff focus on what students can do and provide specific praise and other forms of positive recognition to support social development and long-lasting positive change.

FAMILY INVOLVEMENT: Families provide invaluable knowledge about their children and are essential to an inclusive educational approach. Nest families are an integral part of the team. From their first day, Nest structures and systems encourage ongoing dialogue and partnership between Nest families and the school. Families are involved in decision-making, are updated regularly about changes and progress, and are provided with resources to support generalization and enhance their capacity to help their child as they grow and change.

INDIVIDUAL SUPPORTS: If students don't learn the way we teach, then we must teach the way they learn. While the Nest program's primary approach is holistic and proactive, the use of individualized strategies is considered when necessary. Nest teams meet to surface the underlying causes of the challenges students are experiencing and collaboratively and comprehensively plan how to address the challenges, taking into account the individual neurotype and identity of the child. All individual supports use neurodiversity-affirming practices and remain grounded in our core philosophies.

A Shift in Core Nest Practice

In the section above, we explored the philosophical tenets of the Nest Model that evolved from and underpin what we believe about our students and inclusive education. Based on the foundational beliefs, Nest practices evolved. In traditional special education practice, an assessment team evaluates a student and develops an Individualized Education Program (IEP) that outlines how to remediate the student's weaknesses. The IEP identifies classroom strategies to be implemented for the individual student as well as "related services" to be provided by a therapist, typically requiring that the student be pulled out of class. The services are applied to the student in isolation in the hope that the student will independently apply them across settings. As new challenges are identified, the traditional approach to addressing them is to add more services, and individualized supports are added to the student's IEP. However, more is not necessarily better.

To illustrate this, consider a student named Sonia who needs help learning how to organize her ideas—something that is called an executive functioning skill. In the traditional approach, Sonia might receive Occupational Therapy (OT) services, delivered as a "pull-out" service, to help her address this need. Her removal from the classroom for OT services results in her missing classroom math instruction as well as connection time with her peers. The missed class time causes her to fall behind in math and then need additional support, added to her IEP of course, to help her catch up. This can become an ineffective cycle. Furthermore, providing the numerous individualized strategies mandated by each student's IEP is often impossible for educators to manage in a typical classroom, which may have as many as thirty-two elementary students. Pulled in so many directions, it becomes increasingly difficult for teachers to plan and deliver coherent lessons. This also reduces the positive impact of the OT intervention and Sonia's connection with her peers.

We can imagine the way traditional special education supports students as the system providing a bunch of rubber bands. Each individual rubber band is analogous to a support, service, or strategy that is designed to help the student remediate their problem. But each rubber band works independently and becomes part of a pile of rubber bands on top of the student. The onus to hold the disparate rubber bands together, integrate them, learn from them, and carry that learning across every part of the school day falls on the student.

However, in the Nest Model, the classroom itself is a therapeutic vehicle, meaning the classroom is built in a way that proactively embeds many of the supports that would be listed on an autistic student's IEP into the whole classroom. This holistic approach to environmental and instructional supports provides therapeutic continuity and coherence across the day and across all school settings and creates less need for specific individual supports. This reduces the number of individual management needs the teachers must implement and creates more cohesion amongst peers in the class, as everyone has access to, and benefits from, the embedded supports. Additionally, Nest's collaborative structures enable related service providers, teachers, and administrators to regularly collaborate to share knowledge, brainstorm, and intentionally carry over supports across settings as they create authentic inclusion.

Returning to our example above, if Sonia were to be placed in the Nest program, her executive functioning needs could very likely be met within the therapeutic classroom environment due to the proactive, whole-class supports that are embedded to support student organization skills. Furthermore, Sonia's OT, who participates in the Nest team meetings, is able to provide insight from an expert lens on how executive functioning supports and classroom routines can be implemented holistically in the classroom to meet the individual and collective needs of their students. If Sonia still needed targeted support, OT services would be added to her IEP, and the OT would work collaboratively with the Nest teachers to provide push-in services that model strategies for Sonia and her teachers to use. Rarely, OT services may be provided as a pull-out, but in that case the strategies taught are shared with the Nest team during Sonia's case conference to ensure that all teachers and therapists know about and support their generalization.

In this way, returning to the rubber band metaphor, in Nest, each individual therapeutic service/rubber band is connected via the collaborative interdisciplinary team and related programmatic structures. The collaborative connection itself becomes a vehicle for comprehensively supporting students and embedding carry-over across all settings while removing the onus from the student. We believe this makes Nest a program with "bounce."

There are, of course, always exceptions when a student needs specific individualized supports in the classroom to ensure they have what they need to learn and thrive. The Nest Model provides this opportunity, but because of Nest's collaborative, therapeutic approach, the need for disconnected pull-out services becomes the exception rather than the rule.

FIGURE 4.1. "A Program with Bounce"

The Comprehensive Nest Model

In the early days of Nest, the "Cornerstones" of Nest was developed as a guide to Nest practice. Built directly from that initial work, we developed and continually refined a set of philosophical tenets that drive all of Nest's system-wide structures, inform the collaborative structures that are utilized, and determine the classroom strategies that are implemented. The image below conceptualizes this evolved comprehensive model as a diagram we call "Nest in a Nutshell."

There are four levels of the Nest Model. The top three levels are built on each other, work together, and draw directly from the philosophical tenets on the level below. Each structure and support is grounded in the Nest Model's philosophical foundation. Therefore, to understand the model and implement it with fidelity, educators must understand the new paradigm. Nest is not a model to be implemented mechanically. While each individual structure or practice is valuable, all elements must come together comprehensively and cohesively so that the true impact is realized.

This "Nest in a Nutshell" conceptualization will guide Part II of this book, with the components of the top three levels of the Nest Model being discussed in more detail in subsequent chapters. The original Nest in a Nutshell figure was designed by Aaron Lanou and Dorothy Siegel.

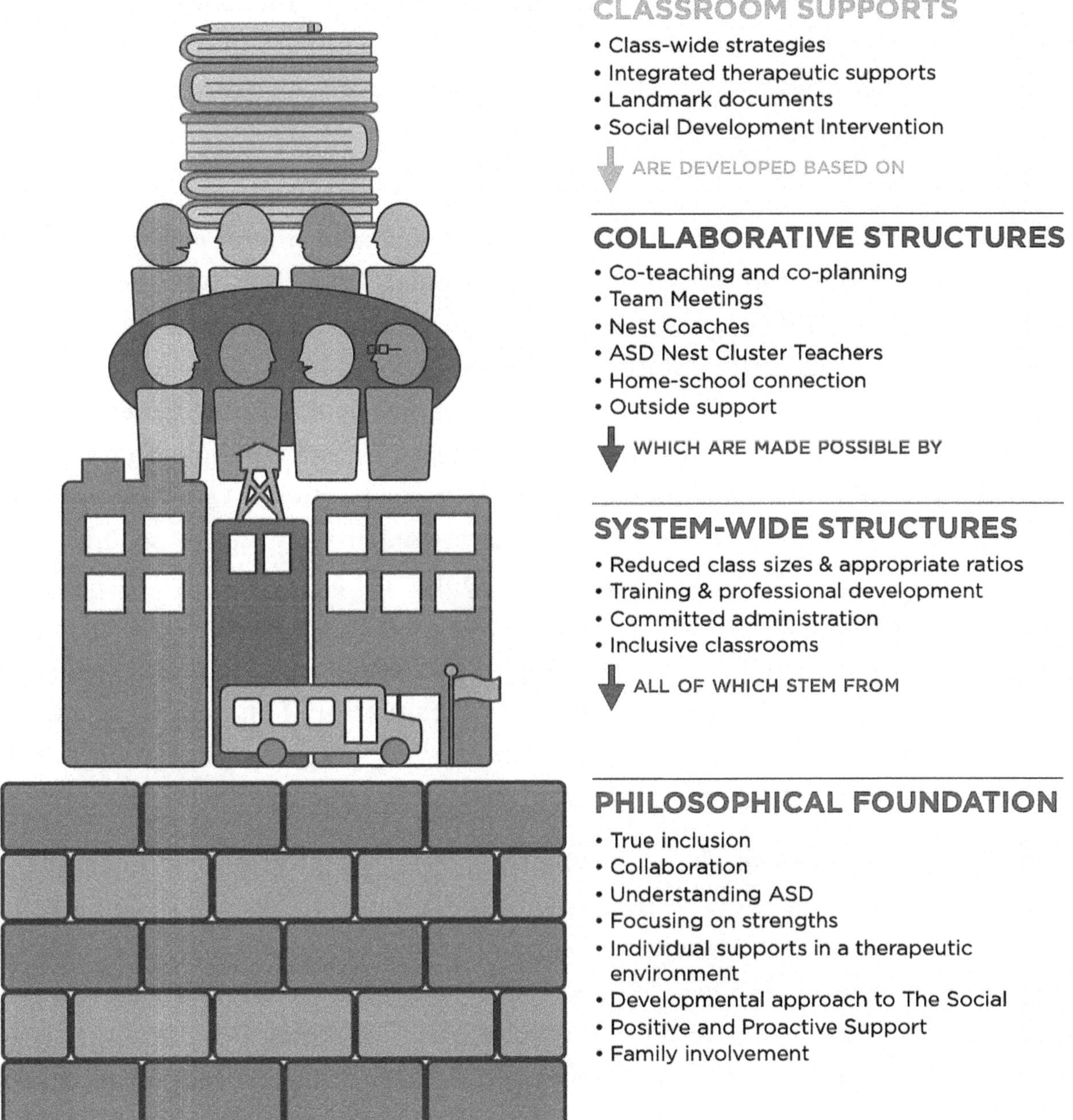

FIGURE 4.2. "Nest in a Nutshell"

Key Theories Guiding Nest Beliefs and Practices

Finally, to understand the philosophical foundations and underpinnings of Nest, it is important to learn about some of the key theories that inform our understanding and practice. The terms and concepts outlined below are integral to the model, are included in our courses and workshops, guide our consultation, and are embedded in Nest resources. They are referenced in the preceding chapters.

SOCIAL MODEL OF DISABILITY: *Social model of disability* was originally coined by the Union of Physically Impaired Against Segregation (*Fundamental Principles of Disability* 1975) to counter the commonly used medical model. Disability rights advocate Alice Wong wrote in *Disability Visibility: First-Person Stories from the Twenty-First Century* that the social model of disability "states that we are disabled by society and lack of access rather than by our bodies." These barriers can be physical, structural, resulting from a lack of access, or attitudinal, such as the belief that disabled people do not have the capability to achieve certain things." This is illustrated further by Cara Liebowitz in her article "I Am Disabled: On Identity-First Versus People-First Language" when she states, "The most basic example is wheelchair accessibility. If I am using my wheelchair and I can't go to a restaurant because it doesn't have a ramp, am I disabled by my cerebral palsy or am I disabled by the inaccessibility of the restaurant? If that restaurant has a ramp, I am able to function perfectly within that situation. I am able to go in, sit at a table, order my food, eat it, and pay, just like everyone else. My wheelchair is not the problem. The inaccessibility of the restaurant is."

According to the social model of disability, it is these external constructs, not the person, that are the cause of limiting full participation in the world. In other words, a disability is only disabling when it prevents someone from doing what they want or need to do. In a Forbes article titled "We Have Been Disabled: How the Pandemic Has Proven the Social Model of Disability," psychologist Dr. Nancy Doyle highlights accessibility, "If everyone was taught sign language at an early age, a deaf person would no longer be disadvantaged. If towns were built and planned with physical disabilities in mind and there was no social stigma attached to looking or sounding different, then having a physical impairment would no longer be disabling." Therefore, if society was constructed in a way that was accessible for disabled people, then everyone would be able to fully engage.

CHAPTER 4

DOUBLE EMPATHY THEORY: The theory of the double empathy problem was developed by Dr. Damian Milton; autistic self-advocate; author; lecturer in Intellectual and Developmental Disability at Tizard Centre, University of Kent; and chair of the Participatory Autism Research Collective (PARC). The double empathy theory (DET) challenges the previous beliefs about theory of mind (TOM). TOM is the ability to attribute mental states to ourselves and others, serving as one of the foundational elements for social interaction, which historically has been attributed as a strength for non-autistic people and a challenge for autistic individuals. However, "The idea that autistic people lack empathy is a damaging stereotype that isn't supported by research. Self-advocates have consistently said that we have different communication styles from others, not a lack of empathy" (Laushman 2022). The theory of the double empathy problem suggests that when people with different neurotypes, or very different experiences of the world, interact with one another, they will struggle to empathize with each other or take each other's perspective. Dr. Milton states, "For a long time, research has shown that autistic people can have trouble figuring out what non-autistic people are thinking and feeling, and this can make it difficult for them to make friends or to fit in. But recently, studies have shown that the problem goes both ways: people who are not autistic also have trouble figuring out what autistic people are thinking and feeling! It is not just autistic people who struggle" (Milton 2018). Conversely, research shows that people are more likely to empathize with those in their in-group (Bennett 2019), meaning those with similar experiences or the same neurotype are more likely to be able to understand each other's perspective. DET encourages us to recognize that the focus should not be on helping autistic people understand non-autistics, but instead it is mutual work in which non-autistics recognize their limitations and work to understand the perspectives of, and empathize with, autistic folks.

SELF-DETERMINATION THEORY: Self-determination theory, developed by Richard Ryan and Edward Deci, is a research-based theory of human motivation in social contexts (Deci and Ryan 1985). As Ryan stated, "We've always been interested in factors that facilitate or undermine that motivation, and in investigating that, we came on the idea that there are some really basic psychological needs that everybody has, whether they're in the classroom, workplace, or sports field, that help them thrive and have their highest quality motivation. Those basic psychological needs are autonomy, competence, and relatedness. That's the theory in a nutshell." People must experience all three needs: autonomy, the need to have choicefulness and control of one's own life; competency, the need to gain mastery and effectiveness; and relatedness, the need to have connection and belonging with others, for autonomous motivation to occur. While people can be extrinsically motivated, for example by money, rewards, grades, or attention, which Ryan and Deci refer to as "controlled motivation," this theory asserts that optimal outcomes occur through autonomous motivation.

Autism and teaching are ever-changing fields. At Nest, we proudly reflect, reconsider, and rethink what we know in order to grow. As lifelong learners, we evolve our model and continually strive toward a world that inherently embraces its neurodiversity. Our model has evolved over the past two decades; we anticipate further evolution as we continue to learn, grow, and be responsive to the world around us, and especially to those we serve.

CHAPTER 5

System-Wide Structures

Allison Graham Brown

The Nest Model is a comprehensive approach to inclusive education. However, it is not a cookie-cutter model, implemented with exact specifications. It is a structured model designed to be responsive to different school communities, cultures, and needs. The responsive nature of the model enables and supports implementation across forty-four different elementary schools in the NYC public school system as of 2024, with those schools varying in size, culture, priorities, resources, and populations served. In order to implement the model with fidelity in this multiplicity of school settings, we developed a comprehensive, flexible framework: the "Nest in a Nutshell" (see chapter 4).

Nest's systemwide structures arose directly from the philosophical tenets that form the model's foundation. These structures define basic Nest protocols that allow the flexibility to respond to the varying needs of the communities and schools being served. Established at the beginning of the Nest Model's development, these systemwide structures remain in use today.

In order for Nest's system-wide structures to be implemented with fidelity, district and school leadership are required to make certain commitments about class organization and composition as well as staff organization. NYCPS provides additional funding to support system-wide structures such as reduced class size and staff compensation for participating in after- or before-school team meetings. NYCPS contracts with the NYU Nest Support Project to provide system-wide structures such as pre-service training, professional development, and ongoing school site consultation. Principals and assistant principals are responsible for securing buy-in from staff, families, and the broader school community. It is through the implementation of these system-wide structures with fidelity that Nest's foundational concepts are realized.

Inclusive Classes

Integrated Co-Teaching (ICT) is a fundamental structural element of the Nest Model. Co-teaching is the sharing of responsibility and instruction for all learners between a general education teacher and a special education teacher in a classroom composed of general education and special education students. The Nest Model has a type of ICT classroom in which the only special education students are students with an autism classification on their IEPs. The ICT structure provides time for the professionals to co-plan and jointly deliver instruction using a variety of approaches whose selection is based on student needs and instructional intent (Friend & Cook 2012). School administrators provide teachers with the time to collaborate and plan their instruction with all learners in mind. The NYCPS provides funding to implement the ICT model in all Nest content classes. Additionally, a Nest cluster teacher (see chapter 6), who is a Nest-trained special education teacher, collaborates with out-of-classroom teachers, often referred to as elective, special, or cluster teachers (e.g., art, music, physical education) to maintain continuity of Nest supports and co-teaching structures in those settings. The use of two highly trained professionals working together in the classroom typically eliminates the need for paraprofessionals or aides.

Program Scheduling

In addition to co-teaching, the Nest elementary model has other systemwide structures that necessitate thoughtful programming. Principals ensure that each program element has a designated space, Nest staff assigned for implementation, and programming scheduled across the year.

Nest team meetings: Principals determine a day and time for the interdisciplinary Nest team meetings, which take place weekly across the school year. To ensure practitioner buy-in and availability, principals gather input from their Nest team to inform scheduling. Practitioners should be informed of the Nest Team Meeting schedule prior to the start of the year so team members can plan their regular attendance. Principals follow NYCPS guidance on the use of the funding allocated by NYCPS to provide per-session payments to staff attending team meetings. (See chapter 6 for details about Nest team meetings.)

Lunch Coverage for Students: A Nest-trained staff member is assigned to support Nest students during lunch and recess. In kindergarten, and in later grades as needed, Nest students receive Instructional Lunch (See chapter 6 for details), which requires a designated alternative location for Nest students during lunch.

Social Development Intervention (SDI): Nest classroom teachers participate in SDI sessions along with their students and a Nest speech provider. (See chapter 9 for details about SDI.) SDI is held in a separate, private location. The Nest students from a class travel to SDI together. Therefore, the session is typically composed of a group of four to five autistic students. Principals create a schedule that enables the special education and general education teachers to take turns participating in SDI, while the other remains with the non-Nest students in the classroom. Kindergarteners receive SDI once per day, and grades one through five receive SDI three times a week. Ideally, SDI occurs at a consistent time in the morning for optimum engagement, and Nest students do not miss core instruction. Here is a sample schedule for a Nest kindergarten class:

Class K-203	Monday	Tuesday	Wednesday	Thursday	Friday
Period	Period 2 9:00-9:45 AM	Period 3 9:45-10:30 AM	Period 2 9:00-9:45 AM	Period 3 9:45-10:30 AM	Period 2 9:00-9:45 AM
SDI Session **SLP** **Room 112**	Ms. Moore (GenEd teacher) Nest Students	Ms. Davis (SpEd teacher) Nest Students	Ms. Moore (GenEd teacher) Nest Students	Ms. Davis (SpEd teacher) Nest Students	Ms. Moore (GenEd teacher) Nest Students
Independent Practice & Small Group Instruction **Room 203**	Ms. Davis (SpEd teacher) Gen Ed Students Math	Ms. Moore (GenEd teacher) Gen Ed Students Reading	Ms. Davis (SpEd teacher) Gen Ed Students Math	Ms. Moore (GenEd teacher) Gen Ed Students Reading	Ms. Davis (SpEd teacher) Gen Ed Students Math

FIGURE 5.1. Sample kindergarten Nest schedule for SDI

Reduced Class Size

Studies have shown that reduced class size can positively impact test scores (Kruger, 1999) as well as provide other benefits, such as increased class engagement (Dee and West 2011). Additionally, most teachers maintain that smaller class size boosts student achievement. In fact, a survey of over ten thousand teachers by Scholastic and the Bill and Melinda Gates Foundation found that nine out of ten teachers believe that to be true (America's Teachers on the Teaching Profession 2012). Small class size and lower student-to-teacher ratios have a significant impact on autistic learners. In Nest classes, there are fewer students in the class and a lower ratio of special education and general education students. For example, in typical inclusion classes, requirements from New York State Department of Education allow up to twelve students with IEPs in an ICT classroom, but in Nest classrooms, the number of students with IEPs is much lower (Continuum of Special Education Services for School-Age Students with Disabilities 2024). Additionally, the total class size is lower than NYC's average, which was 22.6 students per K–5 class in the 2022–2023 school year, according to the data released by NYC Education Department (NYCED 2023). The following are the maximums for Nest classrooms:

- Kindergarten: no more than twelve students (four autistic students)
- Grades 1–3: no more than sixteen students (four autistic students)
- Grades 4–5: no more than twenty students (four to five autistic students)
- No other students with IEPs are in Nest classrooms

Pre-Service Training

Pre-service training for new Nest program staff, including administrators, teachers, and related service providers, takes the form of two foundational college-level courses. The first is an introductory course on autism and the Nest program basics. The second focuses on understanding behavioral theory and its application to the Nest classroom. In both courses, there is a focus on deepening practitioner understanding in the area of autism and inclusion while also familiarizing participants with specific Nest program elements and their applications. These courses help new Nest practitioners become knowledgeable about the philosophical foundations, guiding theories, collaborative structures, and especially the application of the "Elementary Guide" (outlined in chapter 7) of the Nest Model. These courses provide the shared understanding upon which the program is built.

From the start of the Nest program through 2020, Hunter College provided two pre-service courses, SPEDE 771 and SPEDE 772, in the summer semester, with students earning three graduate credits per course. Beginning in 2016, NYCPS contracted with the NYU Support Project to design a fully remote option for the pre-service courses, NYU 701 and 702. These remote courses provide participants with continuing education credits upon completion and are offered in fall, spring, and summer semesters. Since 2021, NYU has provided all pre-service training. The cost of tuition, enrollment, books, and associated fees are covered by NYCPS funding.

Additionally, there is a four-day training course in the summer focusing on Social Development Intervention (SDI) for Speech and Language therapists. (See chapter 9.) SDI, which is unique to the Nest Model, highlights the theoretical and research bases for this intervention and the tools that guide its implementation. Speech providers are the only staff members required to take this course, since they are the primary facilitators of the intervention and receive American Speech-Language and Hearing Association (ASHA) continuing education credits for completion. However, a teacher training course is offered as professional development during the year to support the collaboration between teachers and therapists and support the generalization of social learning in the classroom. The new-to-Nest SLPs then join the New SLP cohort, which meets around five times across their first year in the Nest program. The cohort provides a space for new providers to review the fundamentals of SDI, share their experiences in their first year of delivering the model, and expand their "toolbox" of therapeutic strategies.

New-to-Nest administrators, whether launching a new Nest program or joining a seasoned Nest school, have a one-day training session tailored to leadership building for Nest programs. The bulk of the one-day training is focused on the system-wide and collaborative structures that the principal is charged with setting up, and ensuring implementation with fidelity. The new Nest administrators then become a cohort and engage in three seminars across their first year. These administrators receive targeted support, collaboratively problem solve, and build community with other administrators who are also navigating the early days of being a Nest program leader. Administrators gain practical information as well as being linked into a supportive network that will serve them and their school community throughout the years.

At the end of each semester, an anonymous course evaluation is distributed to participants of the pre-service courses to assess their impact and gather feedback on any areas that could be strengthened (See chapter 12 for their responses).

Ongoing Professional Development

Each year the Nest Support Project develops and facilitates professional development (PD) for Nest program staff. The goal of Nest professional development, another fundamental element of the ASD Nest Model, is to provide staff with continuing learning opportunities to increase their professional knowledge and help them better serve their students. Through professional development, the model aims to broaden and strengthen the expertise of all Nest school-based staff while also creating a community across Nest program schools. The PD program includes opportunities to explore new research and field knowledge, share best practices, facilitate problem-solving, and apply new learning and skills. Professionals collaborate across Nest schools, making connections, sharing experiences, and learning together. The specific goals of the PD program are as follows:

1. Help new Nest professionals make the Nest paradigm shift so they understand the model's foundation that informs the structures and practices they use
2. Update and further expand the knowledge base of experienced staff in the program
3. Build internal capacity within program schools
4. Assist staff in understanding how to support students across their developmental arc and as they advance through the grades
5. Work toward normative coherence across the program schools

Principals at all schools commit to releasing staff to participate in these ongoing PDs. Additionally, time is set aside during school team meetings for staff members who attended Nest PDs to share the information and strategies they learned at these workshops. Principals also provide time for co-teachers to collaborate and plan their instruction with all learners in mind. Principals build planning time into teachers' schedules on a weekly basis during school hours to ensure co-teachers can meet together.

Since 2020, workshops have been provided in a hybrid format. Some are full-day in-person sessions at the NYU Washington Square campus, while others are two-hour Zoom sessions. This hybrid approach has enabled more teachers to participate in PD activities and has provided flexibility for schools to manage coverage when teachers engage in PD.

PD topics are informed by developments in the model, feedback from school staff on needs and interests, observations from consultation in schools, contributions from the autistic advocate community, and advancements in research from the field. Since the program started, professional development has been provided in both one- or two-day workshops on a particular topic, for example executive functioning and co-teaching, as well as ongoing seminars for specific professional staff, such as occupational therapists and social workers. Over time, Nest PDs have been further categorized to respond to the vastly different needs of Nest staff as they establish their years-long careers in Nest. This current categorization, established in 2016, has four levels of workshop offerings, as well as seminars for specific professions.

100 Level

Level 100 workshops are introductory, providing the basics of the Nest approach. These PDs are for all staff new to Nest and those who have not previously taken these workshops. They provide foundational knowledge and skill development. For this reason, the 100 Level workshops are repeated each year and are prerequisites for taking 300 and 400 level workshops. Executive Functioning (EF) and SDI Teacher Training (SDITT) are the two foundational workshops categorized at the100 Level:

Executive Functioning (EF): This workshop provides information about the complex set of cognitive skills that comprise executive functioning and enable us to perform tasks and reach goals. This workshop leads attendees through an exploration of each EF skill and specific strategies and supports to help students develop or strengthen these skills. This workshop deepens awareness of executive functioning skills and the impact they have on learning and engagement, and encourages proactive planning of the classroom environment and instruction to support the development of EF skills.

SDI Teacher Training: This workshop is designed for Nest teachers to learn about Social Development Intervention (SDI), which is a unique approach to supporting students' social development, designed especially for the Nest program. This workshop outlines the approach and strategies used in SDI, with a focus on teacher application in the classroom. This foundational workshop is designed to bolster collaboration between the SLPs and Nest teachers, support the generalization of students' social learning, and support teachers' implementation of social supports in their classrooms.

Level 200

Level 200 workshops provide educators with additional support in particular areas of their work in Nest schools. These workshops have no prerequisites and are open to all Nest program staff. Some of the Level 200 workshops are repeated regularly in response to an identified, ongoing need as staff enter the program, such as Co-Teaching and Understanding & Responding to Challenging Situations. Other workshops are novel each year, in response to the changing field and to areas of interest and need we identify from the surveys and evaluations completed by Nest program staff. Examples of these novel workshops include Autism and Queerness, Academic Supports, and Healing-Centered Classrooms. Here is a brief description of two workshops from this level:

Understanding & Responding to Challenging Situations: Challenges arise naturally in learning environments, despite how predictable we try to make them. This workshop helps participants develop a deeper understanding of behavior and how students can work through challenges in a meaningful way. We discuss how to move away from compliance-based systems, build student's capacities, and problem-solve challenges collaboratively.

Understanding Autism and Queerness – A Journey of Intersectionality: This workshop explores the intersection of autism and queerness and delves into the unique experiences and perspectives of individuals who identify as both autistic and queer. Through an inclusive and compassionate lens, we seek to foster a deeper understanding of challenges and learn helpful strategies to address these challenges with our school community.

Level 300

Level 300 workshops, which focus on new topics every year, deepen educators' practice in their classrooms. These workshops are designed for more seasoned Nest teachers. Prerequisites are the Level 100 workshops, Executive Functioning and SDI Teacher Training, to be completed prior to registering for any Level 300 workshop. Level 300 workshops expand foundational knowledge, deepen understanding, and enhance skills on advanced topics. Workshops that have been offered in this category in recent years include De-escalation, Self-Advocacy and Interdependence, Less Stress & More Bandwidth, Neurodivergence, Intersectionality, and Child Development. Additionally, each year the Nest program has a theme that guides our PD and consultation; a Level 300 workshop is based on the annual theme. Here are brief descriptions of two Level 300 workshops:

Neurodivergence: This advanced workshop helps participants recognize common co-occurring conditions and complex concepts within the autistic and neurodivergent community. Participants will deepen their knowledge about neurodiversity and learn approaches responsive to individual needs, to build relationships, and to work with their team to create inclusive school communities. Participants explore and discuss effective strategies to support learners and are provided with resources to implement immediately and strategies to build throughout the year.

Self-Advocacy and Interdependence: This workshop focuses on the foundations of self-advocacy, specifically considering implications from a disability justice perspective. Participants will learn how to support students through the process of self-advocacy and strategies to foster interdependence amongst autistic students.

Level 400

There is one Level 400 novel workshop per year, designed for experienced, motivated staff who are interested in engaging in a more intimate seminar setting. Both an elementary and a secondary workshop version are offered. This workshop takes place over two full days and requires additional readings and other work engagement both before and between the two sessions. The topic of the 400 Level workshop is the annual Nest theme of the year. The 400 Level workshops are designed to have fewer participants, and facilitation centers on discussions and group work applications. Due to the nature of this workshop, participation requires the completion of a short application along with the usual Level 100 prerequisites. This takes what is presented in Level 300 and expands and deepens the learning and application. Themes from past years have included Connection, Interests, Belonging, Neurodiversity, and Partnership.

Partnership: Nest's theme for a recent year was Partnership. At Nest schools, partnerships are cultivated across multiple settings: between members of the school team, alongside families, and with students themselves. In this seminar, we drew ideas from Dr. Damian Milton's double empathy theory on how to strengthen and deepen the quality of these essential partnerships and broaden the theory's application to school communities. Through this lens, we help foster self-advocacy, navigate challenges, prioritize interests, and enrich social engagement.

FIGURE 5.2. Image designed by Lauren Melissa Ellzey for the Nest theme 2023–2024

CHAPTER 5

Specialist Seminars

A series of specialist seminars are offered every year. These recurring meetings are designed for staff working in particular roles, including administrators, speech providers, occupational therapists, Nest clusters, Nest coaches, social workers, and guidance counselors. To provide authentic expertise and experience, specialist seminars are led by facilitators holding the same license as the participants, and often have autistic advocates as guest speakers or co-facilitators. These seminars provide a unique opportunity to engage in ongoing professional development with colleagues in the same discipline around topics relevant to your specific role. Topics for these sessions are novel, drawing on updates in the specific field and their application to Nest. Practitioners engage in discussions to apply what they have learned, share their experiences, and problem solve collaboratively. Specialist seminars foster community across Nest program schools and enable practitioners to learn from each other. Additionally, these seminars encourage continual reflection and refining of our practice. Nest Support Project facilitators share evolutions to the Nest Model, concepts, practices, and structures, and support implementation of those updates across all Nest schools.

The Nest Coach Seminar series is one of the Specialist Seminars Series. (See chapter 6 for information on the Nest coach role.) These seminars provide direct support to the Nest coach from each school. They meet five times a year with the director of Consultation on the NYU Support Team to build internal capacity at Nest schools. Seminars provide training in leadership development and coaching practices, as well as presentations on program-wide initiatives, advancements in the field, and presentations for autistic advocates. Coaches learn from each other, share best practices, and problem-solve around case studies and challenges they are experiencing. Consultants for each school work directly with the coach during consultation to bridge the seminar work into practice at their school and continue to cultivate the coach role to best support their Nest team and students.

A seminar is held annually for all Nest principals and assistant principals, led by leadership consultants from the NYU Nest Support Team, many of whom are experienced and successful retired Nest school principals. At this meeting, school leaders have an opportunity to share and learn from one another. This seminar does the following:

- Brings school leaders information about new Nest initiatives, newly developed materials, and upcoming events
- Shares new information and advancements from the field
- Explores current and upcoming budgets for the Nest programs at the schools
- Solicits principals' ideas to improve support for their school's implementation of the Nest program
- Shares student and staff successes and outcomes

Illustrious Visitor Presentation

Annually, the Nest Support Project provides an opportunity for a few Nest staff members at each school to attend a workshop by an autistic advocate or other nationally recognized professional in the field of inclusive education. It is a unique opportunity to learn from and be inspired by renowned presenters outside of the Nest program. Attendees are expected to share what they learned at the presentation with their school colleagues during a Nest team meeting. In recent years, Nest staff have learned from presenters such as Dr. Damien Milton, Brenda Smith Myles, Lydia X. Z. Brown, and Paula Kluth.

Ongoing Consultation

The NYU Support Project Team provides ongoing consultation as part of the systemwide structures implemented at Nest program schools. The primary goal of this consultation is to increase the capacity of school-based Nest teams to implement the program with fidelity and support their students. Nest consultation develops individual practitioners' knowledge and skills, enabling them to analyze, reflect, and respond proactively and strategically to support their students. Each Nest program school has a dedicated team of consultants, with varying areas of expertise and training, including autism, inclusion, social development, social-emotional support, behavior support, and leadership. Each school's consultant team develops and maintains collaborative relationships with school staff and provides individual, partner, and group consultation to teachers, related service providers, and administrators, while coordinating with each other to provide comprehensive and cohesive support.

Since 2020, the NYU Support Team has provided hybrid consultation to all Nest schools. By allowing for ongoing dialogue and support, the consultant team can offer in-the-building support and be responsive to immediate school needs. Consultants work with the school team, meet with the school administration, observe students and classrooms, attend team meetings, and often provide mini-PDs specifically designed for the schools they support. The consultation is tailored to the needs and goals of the school administration and of the individual staff members they support in order to meaningfully build the internal capacity of the schools' professionals. New Nest schools and new staff in the program receive ongoing support to develop their understanding of the program, nurture the paradigm shift, and increase their comfort in implementing Nest practices. Consultants also work with experienced staff to deepen and expand their knowledge base, as well as to support shifts in practice aligned with the evolving model. Consultants model and foster true interdisciplinary collaboration across the Nest team that focuses on comprehensive student support grounded in the use of Nest resources, such as "The Elementary Guide." (See chapter 7.) Additionally, consultation helps Nest staff generalize and apply content from the pre-service and ongoing professional development they receive.

Leadership Team Meetings

As established from the beginning of the program, leadership meetings are held at least five times a year with each Nest school. At these meetings representatives from the NYCPS Autism Program Team, the NYU Nest Support Team, and the school administration team come together to discuss program-wide business and provide ongoing support for each school's program. Topics addressed include identifying concerns that may arise relating to implementation of the Nest program; program expansion up the grades; transition to middle school; summer program planning; and examining ways of spreading Nest strategies to the rest of the school.

Onboarding New Nest Program Schools

Once a school has been identified by the NYCPS to become a Nest program site, the Nest onboarding process begins. A series of meetings are set up for the NYCPS Autism Programs team and the Nest Support Project team to meet with school and district leadership. This process mirrors the Nest in a Nutshell format in that it begins with learning Nest philosophy and gradually moves toward the details of implementation in the classroom. An introductory presentation provides the school's administrators and district leaders with a big-picture overview of the comprehensive model, and zeroes in on some of the key philosophical tenets that lay the groundwork for the Nest paradigm shift. From there, working in tandem, the NYCPS Autism Programs team and Nest Support Project team conduct regular meetings with school and district leadership to discuss the commitments required of a school to implement the Nest program, outline the structures and supports available to guide that implementation, and thought partner on each small and large aspect of preparing to launch a Nest program. Meeting agendas consist of assessing the budget, hiring, establishing the collaborative structures, setting up the environment, etc. These meetings take place both in person at the school site to enable building and classroom walkthroughs, and remotely to maintain an ongoing dialogue. These initial meetings establish the collaborative partnership between the school, NYCPS, and NYU, which will continue to be cultivated and remain a constant across the years as a Nest program school.

The onboarding process includes opportunities for new school staff and administrators to visit seasoned Nest program sites. This helps foster relationships amongst Nest program schools as well as offering opportunities for new staff to learn directly from those who have been doing this work. This observation of Nest "in action" allows them to put together all the basic elements of Nest applied across school settings, taking note of the students, environment, structures, language, and approach. New program staff also engage in a question-and-answer session with the seasoned school administration and some other staff members. New staff often find this both grounding and inspiring as they prepare to launch their own Nest program.

While embedding a program into an established school takes time, it is likely to happen faster and more fluidly when the whole school community is primed and provided an opportunity to learn about it. Therefore, another aspect of onboarding is providing an "Introduction to the Nest program" presentation to the entire school community, as well as one for families, to address questions, build excitement and begin establishing a truly inclusive culture from inception. Then, in the summer prior to the beginning of the school year, NYU consultants often join teachers to help them set up a sensory-safe, proactive, and therapeutic classroom to launch their year.

The onboarding process continues across the first year of the new school's Nest program, which includes pre-service training, the Level 100 and 200 PDs, new SLP and administrator cohort seminars, targeted consultation and support to further develop the new team's understanding of Nest philosophy, and the Nest materials and resources available to them on our digital hub.

Learning and implementing the Nest program takes dedicated time and attention. The partnership between the NYCPS, the NYU Support Team, and new schools nurtures the program in each new school, and continually assesses it to ensure that the implementation of the Nest program honors the school culture, enhances their practices, and is done with fidelity.

Conclusion

Nest's systemwide structures uphold the fidelity of the model across schools while enabling the model to be flexible and responsive to the diverse needs of the communities and schools being served by the Nest program.

CHAPTER 6

Collaborative Structures

Allison Graham Brown

In the Nest Model, a common phrase is "the team is the expert." This sentiment draws from the philosophical foundation of collaboration outlined in chapter 4. The team's collaborative processes facilitate the realization of the Nest program's goals. Nest prioritizes and cultivates partnerships across settings: between members of the school team, alongside families, and with students themselves. Collaboration takes place through a series of structures with a variety of stakeholders, at all levels of the model, building off the philosophical foundations and system-wide structures to support the implementation of Nest.

More than twenty years ago, the National Research Council's report, Educating Children with Autism (2001), stated, "Education, both directly of children, and of parents and teachers, is currently the primary form of treatment in autism" (12). That is still, to a large extent, true today. The public school classroom has the potential to become a major vehicle for therapeutic change for autistic students. In order for this therapeutic classroom to be realized, intentional and ongoing collaboration between general education teachers and special education teachers, teachers and related service providers, school and home, and staff and students must occur. The traditional structural silos and boundaries of roles at a school must be broken down, and structures to support collaboration across these groups needs to be implemented. General education teachers who understand and can teach the academic curriculum must be adept at using strategies that work with autistic children, often seen as the exclusive province of special educators and related service providers. At the same time, related service providers need to help their students generalize newly learned skills from their office to the classroom, and they need to collaborate with classroom teachers to achieve that end. The report of the National Research Council also states that the school must support families, whose involvement is critical to their child's success. The Nest Model hinges on collaboration, sharing expertise across key stakeholders and creating the vehicle for comprehensive implementation, to ultimately support the social, emotional, sensory, and academic needs of students.

The Collaborative Team

Each member of the Nest interdisciplinary team has an important area of expertise and individual role, without which the comprehensive nature of the program would not be possible. However, unlike in traditional education settings, in the Nest Model, there is a shared responsibility across settings for Nest professionals, and collaborative structures are embedded to support this transformative approach. Together, these trained professionals work to facilitate Nest students' access to the school experience. In the Nest Model, the team learns from each other, sharing resources and knowledge, to strengthen therapeutic implementation across settings and comprehensively support students.

- **School administrators:** Principals and assistant principals ensure the Nest program is implemented with fidelity in their school. Principals oversee the daily operations of their building, set the vision, and support school staff to enact that vision. Their leadership drives the success of the Nest program by setting the tone for the school community and synthesizing the Nest program into their school culture and vision. Principals are charged with using the Nest budget; conducting Nest hiring; ensuring the scheduling of Integrated Co-teaching, Instructional Lunch, and Social Development Intervention; and implementing program structures. School administrators also support Nest staff by registering them for professional development and releasing them to participate in that training. Additionally, school administrators work closely with the Autism Program Team for the placement of Nest students and working with Nest families.

- **General education teachers:** The general education teacher is the content expert, with training in pedagogical approaches to planning and facilitating lessons, assessing understanding and progress, and adapting curriculum to meet the needs of the student learners. Their knowledge includes the following: understanding child development and learning processes, language acquisition and literacy development, curriculum development and instructional planning, motivation and engagement, and classroom management. General education teachers are trained in Nest and work in tandem with the special education teacher in Nest co-taught classrooms. Nest classroom teachers collaborate regularly with related service providers and cluster teachers at team meetings and throughout the school day to develop and implement academic, social, sensory, and classroom behavior supports.

- **Special education teachers:** The special education teacher provides expertise in understanding disability; developing, managing, and implementing IEPs; and developing and modifying curriculum designed to address student needs and access for all students. In Nest, special educators are equally responsible for establishing a supportive environment, creating and implementing routines, and engaging in classroom management, instruction, and assessment as their general education counterparts. The two teachers work together, leveraging their expertise to co-plan and co-facilitate lessons to proactively meet the needs of all learners and create a therapeutic classroom environment that centers on accessibility and authentic inclusion.
- **Nest cluster teachers:** Nest cluster teachers are Nest-trained special education teachers assigned to a grade or group of classes and support students during out-of-classroom experiences (e.g., art, music, physical education, lunch). The Nest cluster teacher has a comprehensive understanding of autism and their particular Nest students. The Nest cluster teacher collaborates with the out-of-classroom teachers to bring strategies and supports used in Nest classrooms into the specialists' instructional space and activities, with consideration for students' social, sensory, and academic needs. Nest cluster teachers may encourage the use of strategies such as breaking new learning tasks into small steps, slowing the pace of verbal instructions and supplementing them with visuals, and providing opportunities for student choice to support student engagement. Typically, the Nest cluster teacher walks with the students to the other classrooms to ease the transition and provide a routine to ground the students. The Nest cluster is not a teacher aide nor a support for only autistic students, but instead creates a co-teaching dynamic in out-of-classroom settings. Nest clusters also support students during less-structured periods, such as breakfast, lunch, and recess, to carry the therapeutic strategies into those spaces and support full access to those school experiences. Often, Nest cluster teachers facilitate Instructional Lunch.

The Nest Cluster Teacher

Ms. Levine, the Nest cluster, met the first-grade class at the door of their classroom. Franklin, a Nest student, often became very excited during the transition to the art room, leading to running in the hallway. At a recent Nest Team Meeting, the team decided to have students select a movement to focus on when making this transition as a way to support student interest and self-regulation. Ms. Levine greeted the students at their classroom and primed them for the walk. "Good morning, we are going to walk to the art room next to our line partners. We will use our voices at volume number 2, soft voice/whispering. It's Valerie's turn to choose how we move to the art room. Valerie, how should we walk today?" "We should be floating clouds," replied Valerie. "Great idea! Please show us how that might look." After Valerie demonstrated, Ms. Levine said, "I think the cloud is tired today because it has to carry so much rain water, so let's move the cloud slowly. Upon arrival at the art room, the art teacher, Mrs. Lopez, greeted the class at the door holding a chart that Ms. Levine had encouraged her to create to support the entry routine. The chart had numbered steps with specific instructions, each paired with a photo of a student performing the step. Mrs. Lopez read the chart as Ms. Levine pointed to each step. Then Mrs. Lopez welcomed the students to the art room and began the activity for that period.

- **Speech therapists:** According to the NYCPS, "school-based speech and language services are designed to help students develop listening and speaking skills. Goals may address auditory processing (understanding and using the sounds of language), phonological skills (organizing speech sounds), comprehension (understanding language), articulation (forming clear sounds in speech), and social language skills" (schools.nyc.gov). In the Nest program, Speech and Language Pathologists (SLPs) also lead the planning and implementation of Social Development Intervention (SDI) sessions. SLPs collaborate with classroom teachers or Nest clusters during the SDI sessions to encourage generalization in the classroom so SDI sessions are responsive to the needs identified in the classroom setting. Nest SLPs receive specialized training annually in SDI to support their facilitation of SDI lessons as well as strengthen their capacity to support their Nest team in understanding the social and communication needs and supports of their autistic learners. SLPs are responsible for turn-keying the

SDI Explorations to the Nest staff and for guiding and monitoring the completion of the Wayfinder and SDI Team Planning Maps throughout the year. (See chapter 9 for explanations of these concepts.)

- **Social workers and guidance counselors:** The Nest counselor has two primary roles, being the lead professional to liaise with and support Nest families and provide the social-emotional lens on the Nest team. This relationship is established at the home visit and continues with regular communication with each family. The counselor presents the family's questions and concerns at team meetings and shares what they've learned about the family's cultural and intersectional identity of the child, home experience, and values and goals. Additionally, the Nest social worker/guidance counselor facilitates Nest family meetings and workshops at least four times a year and acts as a resource for Nest families. Due to their field expertise and training, the Nest counselor provides the social-emotional lens to the team. They may work directly with students to help them understand and manage their emotions, develop healthy relationships, and make informed choices. They also guide the Nest team to understand and support the mental health, social-emotional development, and co-occurring conditions of their Nest students. While there are no programmatic mandates for counseling in Nest, Nest counselors provide individual and/or group school counseling sessions as outlined on students' IEPs. The NYCPS outlines the role of counseling services in school as follows: "Help students improve their social, emotional, and coping skills. Goals may address appropriate school behavior and self-control, peer relationships, conflict resolution, and low self-esteem" (schools.nyc.gov).

- **Occupational therapists:** In Nest, occupational therapists (OTs) provide expertise in understanding the sensory and regulation processes and needs of students. Nest OTs support students to develop self-awareness and self-regulation, with the goal of interdependence, while also supporting Nest staff to consider their environment and routines to cultivate sensory-safe classrooms. OT's are part of the team and participate in team meetings regularly.

  Occupational therapy services emphasize independence in activities of daily living and skill acquisition. They support school participation across settings. OT is not a programmatic mandate in Nest, but OTs may provide individual and/or group sessions as outlined on students' IEPs. The NYCPS outlines the purpose of occupational therapy as follows: "Maintain, improve, or restore function of students in all education-related activities, including neuro-musculoskeletal function; motor function including fine motor, oral motor, and visual motor integration; sensory and perceptual function; cognitive, and psychosocial function." (https://www.schools.nyc.gov/careers/other-jobs-in-schools/occupational-and-physical-therapists, May, 2024).

- **Nest Coaches:** As part of the Nest Model, the NYU Nest Support Project provides specific additional training and mentoring of identified Nest Coaches to increase the level of professional expertise and deepen internal capacity at Nest program schools. During the third year of a Nest program, Nest Coaches are selected by their school administration. The Nest coaches are experienced special educators who receive additional training and support, thus becoming highly qualified "point persons," committed to advancing the Nest program at their schools. The Nest coach is not a supervisory position, nor do the coaches function in an evaluative capacity. These coaches provide support to their school's Nest staff and students and act as liaisons to the NYU Nest Support Project as well as between the school staff and administration. While it is up to each school to determine what the priorities are for their Nest Coach, some common responsibilities include the following:
    - Supporting the implementation of class-wide proactive strategies
    - Working in classrooms supporting teachers and/or students
    - Meeting with teachers and/or related service providers to brainstorm, design, implement, and track the efficacy of strategies or interventions
    - Promoting the generalization of SDI concepts across settings in the school day
    - Providing professional development for their school's Nest and non-Nest professionals to help the school adopt and maintain Nest practices schoolwide
    - Planning and facilitating Nest team meetings
    - Supporting the administration in implementing all elements of the Nest Model

- **Nest families:** Families are experts on their children and are an integral part of the Nest Team. They provide Nest teams with valuable insight on past experiences, family and community culture and values, and current circumstances and priorities. Nest staff work alongside families to deepen their understanding of students as multi-faceted individuals with intersectional identities. Families have the power to bridge learning from school and support the generalization of skills across settings. Therefore, ongoing and consistent partnering between families and school staff fosters a comprehensive approach to supporting the learning, development, and education of Nest students. Family engagement in schools contributes to positive student outcomes, including improved child and student achievement, decreased disciplinary issues, improved family-teacher and teacher-student relationships, and improved school environment (Henderson and Mapp 2002).

- **Nest students:** Students are integral to the collaborative team. As Dr. Ruth Moyse stated "Autistic pupils are best served by parents and professionals working in partnership together ... Central to this conversation must be the views and voices of autistic children and young people" (Wood 2022, 135 & 138). Through open and active communication, guided by the double empathy theory, educators partner with students, fostering self-determinate lives. Nest staff partner with students to understand their perspectives, experiences, and preferences to integrate students' authentic interests into lesson delivery, activities, assignments, and projects. Additionally, Nest teams include students' voices in the creation and implementation of routines, activities, and supports.

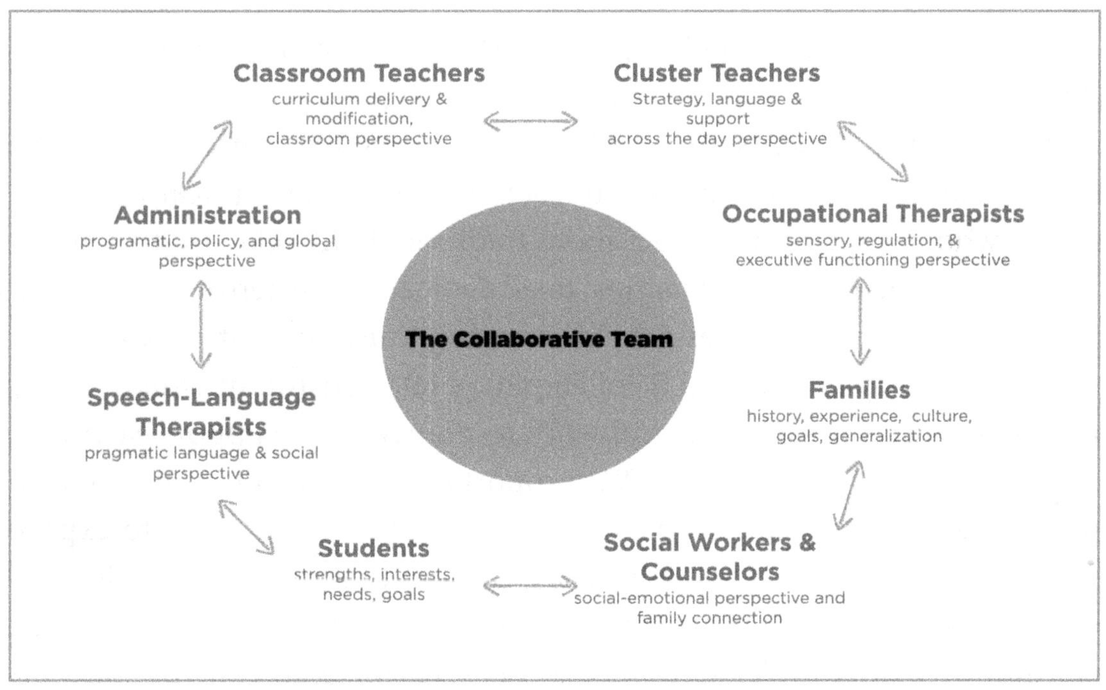

FIGURE 6.1. The Collaborative Team

The Collaborative Classroom

- **Elevating inclusion and accessibility:** Nest uses a Universal Design for Learning (Rose 2001) approach in which educational goals, materials, methods, and assessments are designed to be accessible and meaningful for all students. In a traditional classroom, lessons are typically planned based on the "average" student. Then differentiation is considered and accommodations are provided only to those who have been directly identified as having a support need. This method involves teachers retrofitting lessons to meet learner needs and is often "reactionary," i.e., providing specific support after a student begins to struggle. Unlike the traditional classroom, in Nest, co-teachers work together to plan lessons with all learners in mind from the beginning, and supports are available to all learners. Additionally, driven by self-determination theory, Nest teachers collaborate with students to help them better understand themselves—their strengths and their learning needs—and help them identify learning methods and supports that work well for them. Nest classrooms use a variety of teaching methods to remove any barriers to learning, build in flexibility that can be adjusted for every student's strengths and needs, and provide all students with an equal opportunity to succeed. The Nest Model benefits all learners, creating an accessible, truly inclusive, and collaborative classroom.

- **Co-teachers:** As discussed in chapter 5, Nest classrooms use Integrated Co-teaching, involving two highly trained and actively engaged teachers working in tandem to support all their students. This collaborative approach, with one general education teacher and one special education teacher, involves a significant shift for many educators who are accustomed to a more traditional "my classroom, my students" mentality. Co-teaching relationships take dedication, intentionality, and effort to make the shift and be successful. Co-teaching must be built on a foundation of respect and honesty to establish a collaborative relationship in which both people express their needs, feel valued, and work responsively to support each other and their learners. For this reason, the NYU Support Project consultation and workshops supporting co-teaching begin with encouraging co-teaching pairs to express their core values as professionals and educators, explain their communication style and needs, discuss their own sensory needs, and share their pet peeves. Only after that foundation of shared understanding has been established can the partners work from each other's strengths to determine their workflow, responsibilities, and roles leading to their co-teaching.

- **Co-planning:** Classroom teachers plan together to prepare lessons with all learners in mind. Co-teachers consider their content and students to anticipate potential areas of need and determine supports and strategies to implement proactively. Co-planning requires continuing reflection to consider how previous lessons went and openness to make adjustments so the partnership can evolve and students can thrive. Co-planning ensures that there is a meaningful role for every adult in the room throughout the lesson. Nest co-teachers plan for the following:
    - Environment
    - Student sensory needs
    - Alerting and calming break times
    - Use of visuals
    - Routines
    - Instructional delivery
    - Support for participation and engagement
    - Structures for work in groups, with partners, or independently
    - IEP management needs
    - Supplemental and material needs
    - Data collection and analysis
    - Grading
- **Co-teaching:** Classroom teachers partner to deliver instruction using a variety of co-teaching models, responsive to the needs of their students, the content, and their own strengths. Marilyn Friend and Lynne Cook (Friend & Cook 2012) highlighted six models for the delivery of co-teaching services in the classroom: parallel teaching, station teaching, one teach/one assist, one teach/one observe, team teaching, and alternative teaching. During planning sessions, the teachers discuss the content of particular lessons and what co-teaching model would best fit both the content and the needs of the students, rotating between the different models as appropriate. Nest co-teachers vary the modality of instruction using these co-teaching models to harness the power of the collaborative approach, with both teachers remaining actively engaged in delivering instruction to students. Using a range of co-teaching models enables teachers to have flexible grouping and smaller group size, which in turn supports peer-to-peer connection, along with increased focus and participation.

Nest Team Meetings

Interdisciplinary team meetings are a core collaborative structure of the Nest Model, which drives the Nest program's collaborative approach in comprehensively and cohesively supporting autistic students across the school day and in partnership with the home. Team meetings occur weekly, for one hour, with all interdisciplinary team members in attendance, including the speech therapist, social worker/counselor, occupational therapist, Nest cluster, general education teachers, special education teachers, and administrator. Team meetings typically occur after school, with professionals paid per session for their participation. Team meetings begin the first week of school and continue throughout the school year. A Nest Team Meeting Manual provides an overview of the process, suggestions for team roles, sample agendas, and case conferencing forms. Records are maintained on all topics discussed, for follow-up. There are several components that comprise a Nest Team Meeting, but not all meetings include each element:

Program business:

- The Nest team discusses general school and program business to plan for and support Nest students through any changes that will be taking place, e.g., upcoming holidays, testing, and celebrations.
- SDI Exploration overview and planning: Every other month, the speech and language provider in the program reviews the upcoming SDI Exploration, discussing goals, relevant activities, and SDI vocabulary. Grade or co-teaching teams work with SLPs and other providers to complete SDI Team Planning Maps to ensure SDI sessions are reflective of student needs.
- Nest teams engage in team-building activities.

Professional development:

- Members of the Nest team share information from Nest workshops they attended to expand the core knowledge of other professionals.
- Members of the Nest team share best practices and model the implementation of successful supports to encourage cohesion across Nest classes.
- The Nest team makes Nest supports to be implemented consistently across the school, e.g., a voice scale poster, slide outlining a breathing routine, or break pass.

- Nest teams engage in professional learning to establish shared understanding and enhance their skills. Teams read articles, watch videos, and explore resources on a variety of topics such as inclusive education, neurodiversity, child development, and communication styles.
- The Nest team participates in team-building activities to get to know each other, build trust, enhance communication, foster creativity, and have fun together.

Nest student case conferences:

- Each Nest student is given case conferencing time across the year, and a rotation is established to ensure that all students are discussed on a regular basis. Each case conferencing team has a timekeeper, agenda keeper, facilitator, and notetaker to facilitate planning and productivity.
- Families are part of the case conferencing process but do not attend Nest team meetings. Often, families are contacted before the case conference to see if they have any questions or concerns that they would like the team to discuss. Also, as a follow-up, a Nest team member reaches out to the family to share the progress the team has seen, address any questions they had, share next steps or goals the team is working toward for their child, and any ways the family may want to consider supporting at home.
- All case conference discussions include the following:
    1. Follow-up on previous plans to monitor implementation
    2. Discussion of recent student progress and successes
    3. Discussion of social, sensory, academic, and behavioral concerns
    4. Planning for supports, strategies, and interventions, how to implement them, and which professionals are responsible for implementation. Discussion is balanced to minimize "storytelling" and maximize discussion, brainstorming, and planning.

Case Conferencing – Joy

Joy is a student in a first-grade class in the Nest program. Today she is on the team meeting agenda for the first case conference.

Team meeting facilitator: Let's start by reviewing the follow-up items from our previous case conference of Joy about six weeks ago.

Teacher 1: At the last case conference, we discussed challenges experienced during the transition from the rug to her desk for reading time. Since Joy seemed to get lost after hearing the directions, we agreed to make a visual of the steps to display for the class and reference during the transition. We decided to include images of a cartoon turtle doing each step since Joy loves turtles. We're happy to report that the visual, which we developed in collaboration with the speech team, has helped a lot with the reading routine! Joy is now smoothly transitioning from the rug, choosing a book, and getting started on reading at her desk—it has actually helped a couple of our other students too.

Team facilitator: That's great. Any takeaways or highlights before we move on?

Teacher 2: We've been thinking about how visuals seem to be a great support for her.

Team facilitator: Okay, let's keep that in mind as we move on today. Please make sure it's marked in the notes. How are things going now?

Teacher 2: Joy is doing great in math and has been helping her table when they get stuck. Lately, Joy has been having a lot of trouble producing writing. We started a personal narrative unit, and she listens and participates during the mini-lesson, but when it's time to start writing, she doesn't write anything, and posting a visual of the steps doesn't seem to help.

Occupational therapist: Do you think it might be related to her fine-motor difficulty?

Teacher 1: Well, we still use the slant board you introduced to her, and that has helped. But we didn't see this problem during our last unit on nonfiction, when she decided to write about sea turtles, so it doesn't seem like that's the main issue.

Teacher 2: For this unit, she can write about any true story, but Joy can't think of any ideas to write about.

Social worker: The last time I spoke with her father, he told me that Joy rarely tells about her day at school, and if she does, she explains the details of the class schedule from the day.

Speech-language pathologist: It sounds like the issue might be related to episodic memory—she may not be connecting memories of events with strong emotions, which is what helps to form a lasting, meaningful memory. When we think back on an event from our life, we sometimes call on that memory through the emotion we attached to it. These are our autobiographical memories rather than our procedural memories for a list of facts. For students with strong episodic memory, "Think of a time when you were excited," may cause students to easily recall a birthday party or vacation. If Joy is not forming these connections, then these personal narratives could be particularly challenging for her.

Teacher 1: Come to think of it, Joy rarely shares anything about her weekends during morning meetings on Mondays. She remembers the sequence of events, but she doesn't talk about how she felt or highlight a particularly fun part.

Speech-language pathologist: We could see if the cluster teacher could start taking photographs during activities Joy likes and reviewing them with her. That may help her make these connections in her memory.

Cluster teacher: I could take photos during art and at recess. She loves art and always plays games with other kids at recess.

Social worker: That's a great idea! I can also reach out to her family to see if they can send in a couple of photos from significant events to help her select a topic for this writing piece. It may help her recall the experience.

Teacher 1: Absolutely. Then we can help her decide which photograph she would want to write about.

Facilitator: OK, thanks, everyone. Now we have a strategy. So the plan is to have the cluster teacher take photos at recess and during art, and the social worker will gather some photos from her family. Those photos will be shared with the teachers so they can be used with Joy during the writing period. We'll follow up on how this is going at Joy's next case conference.

Instructional Lunch

Instructional lunch is a unique feature of the Nest program. Autistic students can find unstructured times with high social demands and sensorily overwhelming environments especially challenging. Since lunch is generally unstructured or only lightly structured, with high social and sensory demands, Nest provides a supportive alternative called Instructional Lunch. While there is no explicit instruction occurring during this time, the Nest students are provided a supportive environment where they feel comfortable and relaxed and have opportunities to connect with their peers.

The Nest Model includes an Instructional Lunch for all Nest kindergarteners, many first graders, and for Nest students above first grade as needed. For younger students, instructional lunch is often held in their own classroom. For older students, the model responds flexibly to students' needs. For example, students may have Instructional Lunch in a small room near the school lunchroom, or Nest professionals may facilitate students' transition into the school cafeteria and support them there.

Typically, the Nest Cluster teacher facilitates instructional lunch and establishes clear and consistent lunchtime routines, supports communication and socialization amongst students, and supervises the students' eating. Facilitation of Instructional Lunch also supports students' pragmatic language, as well as social relational and problem-solving needs to expand and generalize concepts focused on during Social Development Intervention sessions. (See chapter 9.) Often, Nest occupational therapists, speech providers, and/or counselors collaborate in facilitation, providing opportunities to enhance support of regulation, communication, and social-emotional development. Some of the activities in Instructional Lunch are designed to help prepare students to make the transition to the cafeteria, such as visiting the cafeteria when it is not in use and learning about its rules and procedures. Some Nest students may be ready to transition into the cafeteria during their kindergarten year, while others transition in later grades. There are some Nest students for whom the cafeteria remains overwhelming, and instructional lunch in a separate location continues to be necessary. The collaborative team, including the family and the students themselves, make the decision as to when a transition into the cafeteria is made.

CHAPTER 6

Home-School Collaboration

Families are experts on their home community, culture, and values and provide unique insight into their child's experience. The partnership between Nest families and schools is necessary to the success of the Nest program and especially the students it serves.

The Nest school team works collaboratively with Nest families, working proactively and maintaining a professional and open line of communication via phone, email, and meetings. The purpose of regular outreach to families is to maintain ongoing collaboration to cultivate positive relationships with families; record successes and highlights, upcoming events/activities, or concerns; share helpful strategies from school to use at home; share resources related to relevant topics for families; ask/answer questions; and gain insight into family concerns. While the social worker/guidance counselor typically acts as the primary point person for Nest families, all Nest professionals take an active role in communicating and partnering with Nest families.

While Nest families are included in all general school activities, celebrations, supports, and communication, there are additional ways in which the Nest team collaborates with Nest families on an ongoing basis:

- **Home visits:** A home visit occurs anytime a student transitions into the Nest program. This may include students in an articulating grade or non-articulating grade and mid-year transfers. The purpose of the home visit is to establish a relationship and open dialogue between the family, students, and school Nest team, which is nurtured across the years. For home visits, two Nest professionals visit the Nest family. One staff member, typically the social worker/guidance counselor, meets with the family while the other staff member, typically a teacher or speech provider, meets with the student. It is an opportunity for the school staff to get to know the student and family, to address their questions, and to help prepare the student and family as they transition into the Nest school. Information obtained at the home visit is shared with the Nest team during a team meeting to ensure consistency of support.
- **Team meetings:** Often, Nest teams reach out to families before Nest team meetings to gather information from the family to inform the Nest case conference. Then,

Nest teams communicate with families after a case conference about their child to share strengths, progress, next steps, and goals and partner with families to support generalization.

- **Family newsletters:** Nest families receive digital NYU Family Newsletters on a regular basis. New-to-Nest families receive two editions a month in their first year and monthly editions across their second year, which provides foundational information about autism, Nest program structures, Nest philosophy, details about strategies, and resources for families. In addition to the first two cycles, Nest families receive quarterly newsletters with current events, resources, and updates from the fields of autism and inclusion and from the Nest program.
- **Family workshops:** An expectation of the Nest program is for schools to provide quarterly family meetings or workshops across each academic year. The school-based social worker/guidance counselor facilitates these regular Nest family workshops in school or remotely. These meetings are used to encourage and build communication with families, develop and continue a supportive community, inform families about school practices, and provide training and support for families related to autism and Nest supports. Additionally, the NYU Nest Support Project provides at least four family workshops per year on relevant topics such as child development, establishing meaningful routines at home, autistic identity, supporting executive functioning, decoding challenging situations, and co-regulation. At least one of the NYU workshops per year is presented by an autistic self-advocate.

Leadership Team Meetings

Another key collaboration that has been referenced throughout the book is between the school administration, New York City Public Schools (NYCPS) central team members, and NYU Nest Support Project leadership consultants. As discussed in chapter 5, the initial collaboration begins with onboarding new Nest schools and continues annually with all Nest program schools. Nest leadership team meetings (LTMs) are an ongoing collaborative structure in which members from these three groups meet at least bi-monthly to discuss program business and work together toward fidelity of implementation. At times, district leaders participate in the LTMs to support the school.

During the LTMs, each group has specific roles and responsibilities; the NYU team focuses on school consultation, pre-service training, and ongoing professional development; the NYCPS leads discussions on partnering with families, budget and funds, and placement of Nest students; and the school team shares updates and questions regarding their Nest students, program implementation, and staff. Collectively, the three groups collaborate to reflect, problem-solve, goal set, and plan to work toward program growth, progress, and fidelity at the Nest program school.

Here is a sample agenda typical of a midyear Leadership Team Meeting:

Leadership Meeting 3

1. Nest kudos. Share a recent Nest Success

2. Program Check-in

Student Status:
- Nest student progress
- Student register updates

Team Meetings:
- Case Conference check-in
- PD turn-key from staff

SDI:
- Team Planning Maps
- SLP share Exploration with team

Family Support:
- Partnering with families
- Hosting your Nest Family Workshops
- Upcoming NYU Family Webinars

3. Support & Training

Consultation:
- What are your needs?

PD & Training:
- Semester 2 registration & offerings

4. Resources
- Admin Hub link
- Nest Practitioner Hub Link

FIGURE 6.2. Sample leadership meeting agenda

Conclusion

Collaboration is a philosophical tenet underpinning Nest. The collaborative structures outlined in this chapter provide the vehicle through which meaningful interdisciplinary collaboration can occur, making the Nest team the true expert in any Nest school.

CHAPTER 7

Classroom and Instructional Supports

Brandy Stanfill-Hobbs

The final component of the Nest framework comprising our philosophical foundations, system-wide structures, and collaborative structures are classroom supports. These supports include instructional practices, environmental design, and sensory, social, and behavioral supports.

Over the twenty years of the Nest program, classroom supports have evolved to match current research, to reflect the experiences of Nest students and practitioners, and to incorporate and build on the perspectives and lived experiences of autistic self-advocates. Program goals have been expanded to include creating neurodiversity-affirming spaces and classroom communities.

Original Nest Guideposts and Three-Tier Framework

The original Nest guiding documents were based on research and best practices at the time of the program pilot (2003–2005) and the first few years of Nest at the elementary school level. Those documents incorporated positive behavior support within an applied behavior analysis framework. "The Classroom Guideposts" included sections on prevention of interfering behavior, instructional strategies and supports, social supports, teaching replacement behaviors, and positive reinforcement systems, which together served as a framework for program practices, "The ASD Nest program uses a Positive Behavior Support approach, and incorporates strategies that address areas of difficulty common in children with autism spectrum disorders, specifically sensory functioning, social relatedness, self-regulation, managing anxiety, and selective cognitive problems ... the premise of these Guideposts is that school-based interventions can help many children with ASD succeed" (Bleiweiss et al. 2013).

Prevention of "interfering behavior," which was a major focus of early Nest training and classroom practices, included strategies that we now recognize as largely sensory and visual supports. Early Nest instructional strategies included opportunities for student choice, incorporating student interests, priming, and the use of a variety of co-teaching methods. All of these strategies remain in place in the Nest program, now with the focus on supporting student autonomy, providing meaningful opportunities for engagement and learning, and building connection between students.

To support practitioner implementation of Classroom Guidepost strategies, the Three-Tier Model of Supports was created. The tiers were based on RTI (response to intervention) principles and divided Nest strategies into tiers based on individualization and intensity of needed support. Tier I strategies were "basic, class-wide supports for all Nest classrooms" that included access to classroom break areas, reinforcement of positive behavior with behavior-specific feedback, previewing of all new academic content, and frequent reference to a class schedule. Tier II were "individualized, planned strategies" added to Tier I interventions and included sensory diets, task boards, and individualized or simplified graphic organizers. Tier III consisted of "intensive, individual interventions" that required the support of a central Nest consultant before being implemented. Tier lll strategies included frequent, scheduled, teacher-supported breaks, intensive reinforcement systems with teacher monitoring, and supplemental academic programs.

The tiers were organized into checklists, allowing practitioners to track which strategies were in place for a particular student and to make notes on implementation and effectiveness. It was recognized that student needs would change across the school year and that needs would vary across domains—a student might benefit from a Tier III intervention for behavior support while receiving Tier I sensory supports. Levels of support were tracked as evidence of student progress.

A Shift in Perspective and Practice

Over time, Nest practitioners began to recognize, and older students began to communicate, that not all of the behavior-based interventions were beneficial to Nest students. The emphasis on reducing "interfering behaviors" led to attempts at behavior change without a complete understanding of student strengths and needs, which often taught students to mask their autistic traits and accept neurotypical readings of the world as absolute. With the introduction of training on the concept and classroom practices related to neurodiversity in 2015, the program began a significant shift in understanding of autism and its approach to creating and supporting Nest communities.

Soon after, Nest teachers and therapists began incorporating elements of neurodiversity-affirming practice into their work. Contrary to the traditional education approach that has a deficits-based lens and focuses on remediating the differences or impairments associated with neurodevelopmental conditions, a neurodiversity-affirming approach is built on the understanding that all neurotypes have unique strengths, interests, and needs.

Traditional approaches to working with autistic students focus on teaching students to mask autistic traits by, for example, reducing stimming, pressing for more direct eye contact, and teaching communication methods that make neurotypical people comfortable. Recent research demonstrates that these practices can lead to anxiety, shame, low self-worth, and depression in neurodivergent people (Sedgewick et al. 2021). Neurodiversity-affirming practice is built on understanding differences in the way autistics experience the world and adapting teaching and therapeutic practices, along with learning environments in ways that affirm neurodivergent identities.

The second major element that drove the revision of classroom practices is Dr. Damian Milton's double empathy theory. While traditional or ABA-based approaches to teaching autistic students view the communication challenges between autistic and non-autistic people as being the result, and therefore the fault and responsibility, of autistic neurology, Dr. Milton's theory posits that human beings are simply not good at communicating across neurotype. Difficulty communicating across neurotype leads to difficulty empathizing with others with different neurology than one's own, creating a situation where neither communicator has empathy, or a double empathy problem (Milton 2012). When educators recognize their biases in favor of students with their same neurology and against students who think and experience the world differently, classroom environments and instruction can be designed to create a variety of connection points and learning opportunities, rather than requiring that all students engage and learn in the same way.

The final shift in Nest practices that informs current work is the incorporation of student interests. Nest consultants are often asked how to stop a child from thinking about their interest. It often sounds something like, “How do I get them to stop thinking about trains so they can pay attention to math?” Or, “How will she ever make friends if she always talks about rabbits?” The answer is, it can’t be done. And it shouldn’t. The logical and supportive way to work with student interests is to help students identify peers who share their interests so they can build social connections, to make lessons interesting enough to hold a student’s attention, and to incorporate a child’s interest into our work whenever possible.

All human beings have interests that are meaningful and rewarding to engage in. Neurotypical people often compartmentalize these interests, or share information about them discreetly. Many neurotypical people are intense fans of particular television shows, movies, comics, or books and participate in related clubs or conventions. Interest in sports, or a particular sport, is a commonly held interest that may include the memorizing of player profiles and game statistics. It’s common to talk about interests with people who share them. When educators recognize that specific or intense interests are not particular to autistic people but rather are a common characteristic of people, it creates an opportunity to build strong connections with and between students and may help autistic learners build on their interests in ways that enhance their quality of life now and in the future.

In 2022, the NYU Nest Support Project launched the new Classroom Guide. The Guide incorporates the double empathy theory, neurodiversity-affirming practice, and incorporating students’ interests into strategies and practices in four domains: sensory, social, instruction, and behavior support. It is designed to create opportunities for partnership between practitioners and students.

Current Nest Classroom Practices

The goal of the Nest program is for students to learn and develop in a supportive school environment that fosters connection and creates space to explore interests, so that students can grow into happy, fulfilled, self-determined autistic adults. Therefore, Nest structures and strategies are designed to help Nest practitioners support and affirm autistic learners in inclusive settings. Nest classroom practices are proactive, classwide strategies that create sensory-safe, socially and academically accessible, and regulation-supporting learning environments. Nest strategies are intentional "all the time" strategies, meaning that they are built into all classroom and therapeutic practice and are always available to students.

Best practice for supporting autistic learners is to establish foundational Nest practices in your classroom before considering how to implement practices based on a student's individual needs. In other words, Nest practitioners build in access for students ***pro*actively**, instead of providing accommodations *re*actively.

Nest supports incorporate concepts from *Self-Determination Theory* (Deci and Ryan 2000). The Nest program aims to support each student in interacting with the world and ultimately self-advocating in a way that works best for them. Self-determination theory is a theory of human motivation that suggests that the elements of intrinsic, autonomous motivation are *competence* (i.e., feeling adequate about things that matter to oneself), *autonomy* (i.e., opportunities to make choices), and *relatedness* (i.e., caring about and feeling connected to others and feeling cared for). Rewards and other extrinsic motivators are used sparingly. Nest strategies are designed to support students' competence, autonomy, choice, and relatedness.

The cornerstone of the Nest elementary model is the proactive approach to building a sense of safety and predictability and the opportunity to build connection. To this end, co-teachers participate in training that includes executive functioning support; implementation of class-wide sensory, social, instructional, and behavioral supports; the role of a teacher in SDI; co-teaching models; and collaboration. Additionally, classroom teachers co-plan lessons that are designed to be socially and emotionally safe and provide opportunities for connection between students.

Students are primed for novel activities and are provided with opportunities to practice routines with teacher support and gradual release of responsibility before being expected to perform them independently. Once routines are in place and secure, teachers build positive anticipation of new activities by including "surprises" (with a question mark in the daily schedule) and co-regulating with students before and during the class's engagement with the surprise.

Nest teachers take time and great care to build classroom community through regularly occurring structures like morning meetings, community corners, celebrations of group accomplishments, and field trips around areas of shared interest and enthusiasm.

Nest's instructional practices intentionally reflect a *universal design for learning* philosophy. The strategies used support autistic learners in inclusive settings while providing opportunities for all students to meaningfully engage in lessons and activities. They also help practitioners design academic content that is accessible to all the learners in their classroom and to rethink expectations of what academic success looks like. They include the use of a variety of co-teaching models, graphic organizers, and other visual supports, and the provision of extra processing and response time for students who need it.

Universal Design for Learning (UDL) (Rose 2001) is a framework that guides the design of learning experiences to proactively meet the needs of all learners. UDL reflects the position that barriers to learning often exist in the design of the environment, rather than in the student.

Universal Design for Learning may look different across classrooms, but the core elements are consistent. They include the following:

- A focus on building expert learning for all
- All learners knowing the goal
- Intentional, flexible options for all students to use
- Student access to resources from the start of a lesson
- Students building and internalizing their own learning

In a UDL environment, students may not all do the same task at the same time or in the same way. Flexible options will differ across developmental ages, but having clear goals and flexible options is consistent no matter the grade level or content area.

Nest Class-wide Instructional Strategies

Nest instructional strategies are designed to help Nest practitioners support autistic learners in inclusive settings. The strategies are informed by research, the guidance of autistic self-advocates, and the experiences of Nest educators and are implemented systematically by co-teachers and related service providers.

Each of the following instructional strategies includes the "why" of a strategy, explaining the benefit of the strategy to autistic learners, and how practitioners can employ them.

STRATEGY: Structure lessons to promote engagement and align with student ability, with multiple access points for autistic learners.

Why: Learning is enhanced by engaging autistic students through their specific interests and by reflecting their identities. Students are able to make academic gains when they are provided with instruction that balances support and rigor.

How: Lessons include varied access points so all forms of engagement are welcomed and valued. In each lesson, teachers plan for multiple ways for students to participate, including with words, actions, and options for different work products. Students' interests are regularly embedded within content to increase opportunities for engagement and connecting with peers. Instruction is also designed to reflect each student's zone of proximal development, i.e., the point in the learning process between what a student cannot do independently but can do with support, on the way toward mastery of a concept or skill. The zone of proximal development is a valuable area for teaching and learning.

Resources written and developed by diverse authors are featured, to reflect the perspectives and lived experiences of people of different races, gender identities, abilities, and cultures. Neurodiversity is also represented in classroom displays, book choices, and other materials.

Physical response strategies are used frequently to increase student participation, including the use of response cards, whiteboards, gestures, and hand signals. A variety of active learning techniques are used across the day in Nest classrooms, including the use of graphic organizers to support visual processing, executive functioning, and collaborative work.

Movement is incorporated into lessons, through activities such as gallery walks and scavenger hunts, explorations of sensory elements in the classroom, and student-led projects.

STRATEGY: Use a range of co-teaching models to reach the objectives of a lesson and provide varied access points for autistic learners.

Why: Having two teachers in a classroom is a powerful tool to support student learning. This can be especially true for autistic learners because co-teaching methods can be intentionally planned to support autistic neurology and needs. Using a range of co-teaching models enables teachers to have flexible grouping and smaller group size, while maximizing the use of teacher strengths and skills.

How: Lessons are collaboratively planned in advance and reflect the strategic use of co-teaching models. During planning, active co-teaching roles for each component of the lesson are established, and all supports needed are identified in advance and made accessible during instruction. Co-teaching models can be matched to the unique learning styles of students and the particular strengths of the teachers.

STRATEGY: Create classroom routines and procedures that support autonomy for autistic learners.

Why: Autistic learners benefit from predictable classroom environments. When routines and procedures are clear and easy to follow, students are better able to process information, make choices, and engage with peers and teachers.

How: Nest elementary classrooms have a high level of routine and predictability, which help to foster a sense of safety for Autistic learners. Daily schedules are not only posted, but referenced across the day to help students stay oriented and to reduce anxiety about future tasks or the duration of less preferred activities. Nest practitioners create and frequently revisit routines for common academic structures like Think, Pair, Share, or Stop & Jot, and for non-academic routines like entering/exiting routines, packing up, walking in the hallway, etc. Nest students are taught to reference posted lists of tasks they can do if they finish their work ahead of the group. To support access to needed information when students are challenged or in distress, Nest teachers provide and actively teach the use of help cards and non-verbal signals for common occurrences, like a gesture that communicates, "I see that you have a question, and I'm coming to you next."

FIGURE 7.1. What to do when you are done routine from PS 682, Brooklyn

---

STRATEGY: Embed executive functioning tools into lessons and support autistic students' regulation and engagement during independent tasks.

Why: Executive functioning tools are meaningful to support all students' success during independent activities. These supports can increase autistic students' productivity and autonomy, while reducing frustration.

How: Nest practitioners give directions for independent work that are precise and broken into small steps, with visual supports posted for reference. The Nest classroom is set up for student autonomy in accessing materials and tools; routines and use of tools are explicitly taught and practiced by students to enable meaningful use.

Nest teachers model and frequently revisit self-monitoring supports like visual timers, progress bars, and model work samples. Task analyses are used across the day.

STRATEGY: Design lesson presentation for accessibility for autistic and allistic learners.

Why: Autistic learners benefit from lessons planned with accessibility in mind. Lessons that include multiple ways for students to take in content and to express what they have learned support a variety of learning modalities and processing styles.

Research and the experiences of autistic self-advocates tell us that, in general, instructional lectures are less effective for autistic learners. Visuals support understanding and provide a reference that students can access after verbal directions have faded away.

How: When planning delivery of content, include visual, auditory, and tactile support for all learners while adjusting the speed of lesson presentation to account for students' varied processing and response time needs. Pair information that is shared verbally with information that is visually represented by using slides with photos and videos to support lessons. Use 5-point scales to concretize abstract concepts, for example, the intensity ("size") of a problem or a scale about feelings. Use graphic organizers, progress bars, rubrics, and flowcharts to help students monitor their work.

STRATEGY: Provide extended response time for information processing and formulation of responses.

Why: Classroom discussions are inclusive of all students' ideas and perspectives when additional processing time is offered. Autistic learners often process at different rates than their neurotypical peers. Providing extra time increases the accuracy of responses and often increases the number of students who respond as well as the total number of responses.

How: Provide extended time between asking a question and accepting responses. Extending response time reduces student anxiety about processing (thinking about a correct answer) and formulating a response (Nason 2019.). Additionally, visuals that support extended time support social engagement (see chapter 9), while tools like whiteboards and gestures for “same thought” or similar concepts support fast processors to enable them to engage while reducing frustration and calling out.

STRATEGY: Utilize technology tools and platforms to support students’ learning.

Why: Technological tools can increase autonomy and engagement for autistic learners. Fluency with technology prepares students for long-term success in middle school, high school, and beyond for vocational or avocational pursuits.

How: Tech tools are offered as a choice to complete academic tasks and engage in instruction, and assistive tech tools are used as a support (speech-to-text apps, audiobooks, etc.). Tech-based organizational systems such as Google Classroom, Flip Grid, Schoology, and Pear Deck are used to preview new content and support instruction.

Conclusion

The fundamental principle that underlies the Nest classroom and instructional supports is that Nest changes the traditional classroom environment and classroom practices to support autistic learners, rather than attempting to change the child. Nest classrooms and instructional practices honor autistic neurology by creating well-thought-out and flexible intervention strategies to match the neurodiversity of its students and enable them to realize their authentic selves.

CHAPTER 8

Sensory-Safe Environments

Lauren Melissa Ellzey

Carole walks toward the school building, nervous but hopeful. If it were Monday, she might not have made it on the smelly bus, but it is Tuesday, which means that there will be a science lesson in Carole's third-grade class. The sun is out today, which makes Carole smile and twirl a little, because if the sun is out, the class will probably go to the school garden as part of their science lesson. When Carole steps inside the school, she slips off her sunglasses and stares at her feet. The school sometimes feels brighter than the sunny skies outside.

After announcements, Carole's teachers line everyone up. As the class walks through the empty playground and basketball courts to the small garden, Carole breathes in the open air. Once they reach the garden, Carole starts spinning round and round, taking in the big space with her body. One of her teachers tells her to join the class. Carole stretches her wings for a few more spins. Feeling good, she heads to the garden with her teacher.

Everyone has a garden job, but since Carole was late to the garden, her job of tending the yummy-smelling herbs was given to someone else! Instead, her teachers hand her a watering can. Carole doesn't like water. It makes her itchy, especially when it gets on her clothes. As she leans over to water the plants, she accidentally drops the can, and her shoes get soaked!

"I don't want to water the plants!" she tells her teachers. "This isn't fun!"

Students in the Autism Nest program often have similar experiences to the student in the opening vignette. Team meetings are called to discuss the form of the student's behavior, with the goal of identifying the underlying function of the behavior. The interdisciplinary team may ask, "Does Carole have problems with self-regulation? Is she seeking attention? Is she used to getting what she wants exactly how she wants it?" Misunderstandings around the underlying sensory function of a student's behavior may occur because, underneath behavior that may be perplexing to non-autistic practitioners, many autistic students are often experiencing unmet sensory processing needs.

The Nest framework has always considered sensory-processing differences and, over time, has deepened the recognition and support of those needs in the classroom. As the autism research field continuously expands and corrects past misconceptions, and as autistic individuals advocate for ongoing acceptance and understanding, the Nest framework has also evolved. It is important to note the intentionality of language around this topic. For example, the phrase sensory processing *differences* is a purposeful move away from sensory processing *disorder*. The autistic experience is different, not less, and the Nest framework strives toward including and supporting, not curing, different ways of experiencing the senses.

Sensory Processing

Every moment of every day, the brain is managing incoming information from the senses, and then regulating and responding to that sensory input in a graded and adaptive manner. Information is coming through multiple channels, which are often described as the five senses:

- **Visual** (sight)
- **Auditory** (hearing)
- **Tactile** (touch)
- **Olfactory** (smell)
- **Gustatory** (taste)

Beyond these five senses, there are many more. Particularly, there are three additional senses (Hunter 2020) that relate closely to the setup and ongoing narrative of the Nest classroom:

- **Vestibular**, which is housed in the inner ear and is often referred to as the sense of balance.
- **Proprioception**, which informs perception of where the body is and how the body is moving, often referred to as the sense of movement.
- **Interoception**, which supports our understanding of internal bodily cues, such as hunger, thirst, toileting, and heartbeats.

While everyone is processing sensory input and has a unique sensory profile, up to 90 percent of autistic individuals experience sensory processing differences (Passarello et al. 2022). Both the autobiographical (Grandin 1995; Stillman 2003) and empirical literature (Ben-Sasson et al. 2008; Branek et al. 2006; Dunn et al. 2002; Kern et al., 2006) describe the nature of sensory modulation differences in autistic individuals as evident in patterns of hypersensitivity and hyposensitivity to sensory input.

Sensory Processing	Description	Potential Needs
Hypersensitivity	May elicit a heightened response to sensory input that can cause distress, discomfort, pain, or euphoria.	May need the removal or reduction of the sensory input, frequent breaks, access to opt into pleasantly stimulating input.
Hyposensitivity	May elicit a lower level of response to sensory input that can cause sensory seeking or sensory craving.	May need an increase in frequency or intensity of the sensory input.

FIGURE 8.1. Adapted from Wise 2022 and Yellow Ladybugs 2023

Sensory hypersensitivity is often associated with sensory overstimulation and overload. Additionally, there are significant relationships between sensory hypersensitivity and anxiety in autistic children and adolescents (Green and Ben-Sasson 2010; Pfeiffer et al. 2005). At times, autistic students may experience an overwhelming amount of sensory input at a level that is too much for their brains to handle (Wise 2022). Unfortunately, since most other people around an overloaded autistic individual are not experiencing the same level of distress, there may be a disconnect between the autistic student's need for support and the understanding of those who can offer the support (Yellow Ladybugs 2023). It is important to recognize that these feelings of overload are real, as autistic individuals habituate less to visual and auditory sensory input than non-autistic individuals (Jamal et al. 2020) and often show heightened levels of synapses in the brain (Tang et al. 2014).

Many autistic individuals will use coping strategies such as stimming or special interests to self-regulate overstimulating sensory input. In fact, consistent relationships have been found between sensory overstimulation and overload and self-stimulatory or stimming behavior and special interests (Rogers et al. 2003; Wiggins et al. 2009).

Self-regulation refers to a person's ability to regulate their own behavior in response to specific stimuli. It is posited to involve emotional, physiological, and behavioral factors in a dynamic, interdependent system (Calkins and Dedmon 2000). The goal of self-regulation is to maintain their personally optimal level of arousal in each context. Self-regulation is inextricably linked to the sensory environment. More specifically, sensory regulation refers to our brain's and body's ability to adapt to the changes in the environment, be that reducing or raising arousal (Yellow Ladybugs 2023).

Autistic individuals may lean toward being hypersensitive, hyposensitive, or a mixture of both, and these sensory profiles may shift dynamically at different times and in different contexts (Wise 2022). Additionally, while sensory processing differences often involve pain or discomfort and are overwhelming, autistic individuals often share their experiences with positive sensory stimulation, sometimes referred to as sensory joy (Yellow Ladybugs 2023). In the vignette at the beginning of this chapter, Carole experienced both positive and challenging sensory events. Carole enjoyed the freedom of the outside air and tapped into her vestibular sense by spinning, but once the environment changed and she came into contact with a wet tactile experience, she became distressed. Sensory experiences are dynamic, and sensory needs and preferences vary from student to student.

The Active Role of the Environment

Every morning, Jeremiah walks into school with a big grin on his face. He bumps against the walls on his way to class, where he loves eating breakfast at his table in the classroom with two other students. The teachers read stories on the soft carpet, and he loves it when he goes to the table with a few other friends and they play a quiet game with rhyming. But sometimes, the alphabet cards and letters they use are too colorful and the interactive whiteboard is so bright it hurts his eyes. Still, he is getting very good at reading the words.

But then lunchtime and recess get so loud! He feels dizzy on the playground and accidentally bumps into other students. By the time Jeremiah goes back to class, his brain is spinning. The bright lights feel even brighter, and the math games are much louder

> and more active. Sometimes, they have a science lesson, and today, they are making gooey slime. The slime gets on Jeremiah's fingers, and he wants it off! But then it's stuck on his clothes! All the other students are screaming and laughing from the goop, but Jeremiah wants to go home right now!

Environments and our interactions with them can teach us a lot about ourselves. Environments play a key role in how we feel and how we are able to engage in the world around us. A bright classroom, full of reds and oranges and yellows, with lights on and vibrant discussion bouncing off the walls, may be engaging for some, but that may not be how all students experience that classroom. Some students may find a highly stimulating environment dysregulating, distracting, or painful.

Conversely, a classroom can also be a grounding presence. Such a classroom may have neutral colors and pastels that shade the students' eyes. The bustling sounds can rise and fall, supported by voice scales and tennis balls on chair legs and classical music whenever loud activity is taking place outside the window or in the hallways. The students guide themselves or are gently guided to a break area when they start to feel overwhelmed by the day's activities. Alternative seating and fidgets can be made available with clear signage on how and when to use them. In this case, the environment works to mitigate overstimulation and provides tools to support regulation. In this way, the environment can educate students about themselves and others in the same ways that a practitioner might. Overall:

- The school and classroom environment can be considered "the third educator" alongside a co-teacher team (Edwards et al. 1993, 339).
- The school environment is an active contributor to sensory experiences, be it overload or joy (Wise 2022).
- Whether or not a person can sensorily access an environment determines whether that person can engage within the environment, which in turn may influence the person's positive or negative associations with that environment (Jonsson 2022); this underscores the importance of meeting an autistic student's sensory access needs in the classroom and throughout the school.

While some autistic students' sensory needs may be more immediately apparent to educators and practitioners, other students may not outwardly demonstrate their needs. Oftentimes, students may receive a message that they are being "good" when they are not responding honestly to the environment, even if the student is in physical or emotional distress. This camouflaging of an autistic student's needs, in order to gain approval or to not receive punishment, is one example of what is commonly known as "masking." In the words of autistic self-advocate Tanya Adkin, "Much like water, we take the shape of our container. To put it another way, we don't choose the form that our masking takes, the environments we exist within often choose it for us" (2023).

Nest practitioners consider, "What is my Nest classroom environment teaching my students?" In order for the environment to contribute to "a sense of well-being and security in" students, it must be transformed into a space that is "a sort of aquarium that mirrors the ideas, values, attitudes, and cultures of the people who live within it" (Edwards et al. 1993, 339). While this extends beyond the sensory environment, given that physical–including sensory–access may well be the first step toward welcoming and including an individual within a space, sensory-inclusive proactive supports are a foundational pillar within the Nest framework.

With this perspective in mind, the Nest Support Project has intentionally shifted away from the concept of a high-functioning or low-functioning student in a neutral environment. Instead, the focus has changed to exploring the relationship between the student and the environment. There are neurodiverse students in a classroom, each navigating the environment in a way that suits their individual needs. If a student experiences challenges in the sensory environment of the classroom or school—or if it is anticipated that a student will experience challenges—the emphasis is not placed on the student but instead on modifying the challenging environment. In other words, the environment can be adapted to be a high-functioning setting, meaning it functions in a way that meets the needs of the students instead of remaining a low-functioning environment that causes challenges for the students engaging within it. The classroom design must flexibly undergo modification by both the educators and the students so the environment can respond to the access needs of the students (Edwards et al. 1993, 339).

For this reason, the Nest classroom is designed proactively to create sensory-safe environments. Considering sensory joy and also hyposensitivity, a sterile environment is not the goal. Instead, emphasis is placed on curating a balance of sensory input in an active, live environment. The sensory elements of the Nest framework align closely with Universal Design for Learning (UDL). Universal designing involves embedding choices and access for as many people as possible, all with the goal of supporting everyone's independence, social engagement, and well-being (Jonsson 2022). The Nest framework is specifically designed to enhance sensory access to the school environment, which provides choicefulness, safety, and delight to a greater number of students—both Nest and non-Nest. This can be achieved through a blend of the following:

1. School-wide considerations for both low- and high-sensory environments
2. Universally optional access to sensory resources and stimming
3. Movement and relaxation opportunities incorporated into whole-class learning
4. Individualized supports

School-Wide Considerations for Both Low- and High-Sensory Environments

A student's school day begins long before they enter the classroom. Nest students, like all students, wake up in the morning, travel to the school building, and traverse the halls long before they greet their educators at their classroom doors. While a school has limited influence on the sensory experiences a student encounters before that student reaches the school building, Nest schools work to proactively modify the greater school environment, including the hallways, to support students sensorily once they enter school.

Nest schools **reduce visual stimuli** across contexts to minimize sensory overload. In hallways, school spirit signage, kitschy posters, and student work are often displayed in school hallways—all on bright bulletin boards with overstimulating borders. While the goal is not to have an empty, sterile corridor, thoughtfulness can be put into the calmer colors selected for signs, bulletin boards, and borders. Similarly, in the classroom, color choices should veer toward cooler hues with limited decorations, and focus on hanging only the most necessary and meaningful items, enabling students to more easily locate the relevant information they need.

Autistic students are often sensitive to fluorescent and bright artificial lights. Therefore, **adaptations to lighting** in halls, cafeterias, gyms, and classrooms are made. Dimming or partially turning off lights and natural lighting should be embraced whenever possible. Additional lighting possibilities include lamps and single-color, miniature hanging lights.

Some Nest students crave additional stimulation throughout the day. A guided sequence of gross motor movements, also known as a **sensory pathway**, can be built into the hallway. Such pathways are often designed using tape, boxes, and larger tactile materials.

There are so many auditory stimuli to take in during every moment of the school day: student and practitioner voices, scraping chairs, buzzing electronics, and echoes from sounds in the hallways or outside. Supports such as **voice scales** and **muffling materials** on chair legs to dampen noise can make a meaningful difference.

FIGURE 8.2. 5-point voice scale adapted from Buron and Curtis (2012)

Zoning is a great strategy for classrooms, especially those rooms that embrace station teaching. By creating zones, educators can create areas in the classroom that are purposefully more or less stimulating, allowing for more predictability for students. Small groups, imaginative play, and STEM areas may be located in half of the room, while arts and crafts, class libraries, and a sensory safe haven may be in the other.

FIGURE 8.3. An example of a break space in the classroom at PS 206 in Manhattan

FIGURE 8.4. An example of a break space in the classroom at PS 682 in Brooklyn

Figures 8.3 and 8.4 demonstrate how break areas can look very different depending on various factors such as student needs and interests, the availability of space and resources, and the composition of students and staff in the classroom.

A sensory safe haven, also known as a **break space** or **break area**, is located in each Nest classroom and is accessible for all students. Break areas provide a safe space for students to escape overwhelming demands or overstimulation and engage in activities that support self-regulation, which is especially important for autistic students. Break areas are accessed as needed, are non-contingent, and are not a place for direct learning. Breaks are never used as a reward or for a time-out.

FIGURE 8.5. A break area routine chart at PS 75 in Manhattan

The use of the break area is clearly defined for the students, and instruction and practice on how to use it is provided. Students are taught a way of telling the practitioner that they need a break before the student has reached a crisis point. Given the diverse social-communication differences of autistic individuals, a nonspeaking method of requesting a break is encouraged, such as through a break card or a pre-established hand signal.

The sensory safe haven provides an opportunity for a student to unwind and refresh, where otherwise they may continue to experience overstimulation until crisis. The idea of a sensory safe haven can easily be adapted to a variety of spaces and budgets. The steps in creating a sensory safe haven are outlined below.

How to Create and Use a Break Area

A. Designate the area: The break area should be located in a defined space that has boundaries (a corner of the classroom or a separate space divided by bookshelves/furniture, etc.). It is also advantageous to have the break area in a location in which you (or another staff member) are able to keep watch on the student from your vantage point.

B. Gather materials: Consider what you will need to make this space comfortable and inviting as well as functional and safe. Ideas include but are not limited to a small area rug, bean bag, comfortable chair, and/or pillows; a variety of fidgets; timers; break routine/visuals; a menu of options; charts to guide deep breathing, stretching, or arousal exercises; books, music, and drawing materials.

C. Set up: Make sure that materials are easily accessible for students. It is recommended that any optional materials be placed in bins, and label the bins so students know how to clean up the area before they leave it.

D. Introduce: The break area and its use need to be explicitly taught, reminded, and supported. It does not simply *happen*. Explain the break area's purpose and how to use it:

1. Explain its purpose.
2. Review the rules of using it.
3. Detail how to access it.
4. Model how to use it.
5. Explore the fidgets and other materials.

It can be difficult for non-autistic people to anticipate sensory sensitivities, so an environment scan is recommended. This way, general supports can be proactively applied to classrooms before students even step past the threshold on their first day.

Nest Classroom Environment Scan

This scan is a tool to support the consideration of the Nest classroom environment. It is a guide and does not include any mandated supports. The results of the scan can serve as a starting point for environmental supports.

Y = YES; N = NO; S = SOMETIMES

lighting

Lighting can contribute to overstimulation or distraction for autistic learners.

Are fluorescent lights off? __

Are light on/off warnings given? __

Is natural lighting embraced? __

Are laptops closed when not in use? __

organization

Disorganized spaces disallow autistic learners to access relevant information.

Are whiteboards organized? __

Are shelves organized or covered? __

Are charts limited to the day's needs? __

Are materials stored and labeled? __

FIGURE 8.6. Excerpt from the Nest Classroom Environment Scan

Access to Sensory Resources

Even in the best-organized spaces, with well-planned lessons, students may still experience sensory challenges. Autistics, like allistics or non-autistic people, are unique individuals, and therefore autistic sensory responses can vary widely. Different students may crave different sensory experiences or find comfort in different sensory inputs. For this reason, a variety of **sensory resources** are available to students in Nest classrooms at all times. These materials may include fidgets, alternative and flexible seating, noise-canceling headphones, and many more.

FIGURE 8.7. Suggested environmentally supportive supplies for Nest classrooms 2023

These materials should be independently or easily accessible, meaning that students would not depend too heavily on educators to give them the materials they need.

Practitioners should observe for early signs of overstimulation or distress, such as increases in verbalizations, body movements, withdrawal, agitation, or decreased responsiveness (speaking or nonspeaking), and offer materials to students who may still be growing in their self-awareness of both their individual needs and what works best for them.

Another resource that many autistic individuals draw upon for sensory regulation is the natural regulation strategies of their own bodies, namely stimming. **Stimming**, or self-stimulatory behavior, is a method of soothing anxiety, overwhelm, pain, and sensory overstimulation by engaging in repetitive behavior that taps into sensory input (Yellow Ladybugs 2023). While all people engage in self-regulatory stimming, autistic individuals may use it more frequently or with more intensity than non-autistic individuals. Stimming may be an early sign of overstimulation and distress. However, there are also other reasons an autistic individual may stim—to express joy, surprise, and anticipation. Even more, stimming should be seen as autistic body language, as a sign of different emotions along the spectrum of happiness and distress. It should be honored as just as natural as non-autistic body language (Autism West Midlands 2019; Wise 2022).

Stimming may be employed to self-regulate both positive and challenging experiences—including experiences beyond sensory overstimulation. Just as there are numerous neurotypical expressions of emotion, i.e., smiling, laughing, or crying when happy, there are many methods of stimming that express an individual autistic person's experience.

Examples of Stimming Categorized by Sensory Input	
Sight	Gazing at looping visuals (running water, swirling glitter, flickering lights, etc.)
Smell	Breathing in fragrances; smelling food
Taste	Regularly eating spicy or sour foods; sipping drinks repetitively
Touch	Petting or licking items of various textures (soft, rough, bumpy, smooth, scratchy, etc.)
Hearing	Finger tapping; echolalia; singing; listening to the same song/sound in succession
Vestibular	Rocking; spinning; rolling; pacing; toe walking
Proprioception	Chewing or sucking items; leg shaking; hand flapping; squeezing items; pushing and pulling items; bumping into things

FIGURE 8.8. Examples of stimming

In order to ensure authentic inclusion that goes beyond physical integration, Nest classroom practitioners collaborate with students to construct **class expectations**, including language around embracing one another's regulation differences. In Nest classrooms, stimming and the use of sensory resources are a part of the whole-class routine. All students are permitted and encouraged to try out new methods of regulation, such as stimming and utilizing sensory resources and the break area, to learn what works best for them and their bodies.

Movement and Relaxation Opportunities Incorporated into Learning

Given both hypo- and hyper-sensitive needs, Nest students benefit from a range of movement and relaxation opportunities throughout the day. Nest educators regularly schedule whole-class movement and relaxation breaks with the intention of supporting both Nest and non-Nest students (Ridderinkhof et al. 2018; Hunter 2020).

Relaxation breaks, centered on mindfulness, foster focus, body awareness, self-awareness, and emotion regulation (Hölzel et al., 2011). **Mindfulness activities** may include deep-breathing routines, self-initiated compression massage, meditative visualization narratives, and more. While relaxation breaks often occur during transitions, practitioners can weave mindfulness within the lesson, especially if the content is new or challenging. Once a routine is taught and implemented as a whole-class practice, students can also be encouraged to use it individually and in the break area.

How to Introduce a Mindfulness Activity

1. **Introduce** a brief mindfulness activity to the whole student group when they are calm and receptive.
2. **Lead** the activity by modeling the process and guiding students to notice differences in how they feel after mindfulness practice.
3. **Practice** the mindfulness routine on multiple occasions when the students are calm and receptive to ensure a full understanding of the process and purpose.
4. **Use** the activity to help calm or focus all students after a stimulating activity or transition, such as returning from the gym, lunch room, or auditorium, or after several students have experienced frustration.
5. **Individualize** the routine as needed for students and/or encourage the routine when individual students experience uniquely distressing situations. The routine should still continue to be used for the whole class during the key moments as described above.

FIGURE 8.9. Steps for introducing a mindfulness activity

Movement breaks are introduced, led, practiced, and individualized using the same process as shared above. **Targeted movement activities** include practitioner or student-led movements, exercises, movement break videos, or movement-based routines or tasks, i.e. sweeping, wiping down tables, or organizing books and materials. Ideally, movement is also incorporated into lessons as a method for learning. There are a wide range of strategies for **embedding movement into lessons**, such as role play, gestures for key terms, four corners activities, gallery walks, songs and dances for key concepts, and body-based math activities.

Individualized Supports

While the sensory elements of the Nest framework are proactively implemented for the whole class, there may be moments when individual student supports are put into place. Regardless, individualization is not meant to replace whole-class implementation. For example, if lights can be dimmed in a classroom, then dimming the lights would be the first support in place for a student with sensory sensitivities. However, if the lights cannot be dimmed or alternative lighting is not possible, then an individualized support may be necessary, i.e., sunglasses or brimmed hats.

Additionally, sensory materials may be limited, especially as a Nest school begins the process of developing the program. Providing a single set of noise-canceling headphones for one student may be a necessary first step while the school builds its program and acquires sets of headphones for each Nest class.

Individualized support may be needed if a student needs oral sensory input. This student may need individualized **chewable items** that are not shared by others, for example chewable jewelry, chewing gum, and chew rings. Consider collaboration with families, occupational therapists, the student, and the interdisciplinary team when selecting these items. Additionally, individual **comfort items** may provide students with necessary tactile or proprioceptive sensory input that may be hard to emulate through school materials. Invite individual students to bring these items, especially during transition periods or when anticipating challenging situations. Lastly, school policies should be evaluated to ensure that they are not unintentionally limiting students' access to sensory resources. School teams have shared anecdotes of moments when policy itself became a barrier to sensory access, for example prohibiting student comfort items (Kluth and Schwarz 2008).

Many Nest students will also qualify for and benefit from **occupational therapy services.** Once a student has been assessed by an occupational therapist (OT), the OT, in collaboration with other Nest practitioners and the student's family, can formulate a plan for sensorimotor support. The OT will deliver the services in a way that benefits the students and aligns with the student's therapeutic environment. For example, the delivery of OT services may consist of one or more of the following:

- **Consultation:** The therapist provides training to educators and other practitioners on adaptive strategies, i.e., how to make adaptations to classroom environments to support student needs.
- **Group activities: The therapist collaborates with teachers to lead group activities** that support the sensorimotor needs of all students.
- **One-on-one in the classroom (push-in):** The therapist works directly with one student in the classroom to support that student's particular needs during classroom activities. This helps to generalize skills learned outside the classroom.
- **Small group pull-out:** The therapist provides a group session to several students in a designated therapy room.
- **Individual pull-out:** The therapist conducts a therapeutic session with one student outside the classroom to focus on specific supports that the student may later use independently within the classroom and school environment.

For best practice in an inclusion class setting, it is recommended that consultation with educators and other practitioners, group activities in the classroom in collaboration with a teacher, and one-on-one with the student in the classroom during routine activities be tried first (Kuhaneck and Watling 2010). Pull-out sessions should be limited and only used for introduction of a challenging new skill or for practice of a skill(s) that are more suitably developed in private, such as toilet-related support. In Nest, the occupational therapist is integral in establishing sensory-safe school environments and implementing sensory and regulatory supports. (See chapter 6.)

CHAPTER 8

Conclusion

The Nest framework provides supports within four domains: social, instructional, behavioral, and sensory. In many ways, the sensory supports lay the foundation for the other three domains, in that the other domains are areas that are more fully accessed when sensory needs are met. Nest schools incorporate low- and high-sensory environments, access to sensory resources, opportunities for movement and relaxation, and individualized sensory strategies and services, so Nest students can not only access education from the ground up, but also thrive in the school environment.

CHAPTER 9

Social Development Intervention

Susan Ehlerman

What Is Social Development Intervention (SDI) and Why Is It Necessary?

Therapists, teachers, and parents long for the "golden ticket" in autism support. We all want the perfect intervention for the students we work with, teach, and love. We should all want this because this is what all children deserve. However, there exists no one therapy that is perfect for *all* autistic students. Instead, we need to think differently about the adaptability of an intervention from the therapy room to the classroom. We must be realistic about our goals and expectations for children while providing a foundation of thought that is, first and foremost, respectful of the community we support. Then, we must offer a therapeutic model with flexibility built into its core structure: a model flexible enough to mold and nurture the success of every child, which will grow and expand as we better understand neurodivergent brains.

Autistic students are expected to fit into a system of learning that is different from, and sometimes even counter to, their way of thinking. Beyond the typical academic expectations of school, these students must read an invisible language that is not directly taught. Although educators and peers may fluently speak it, they do not need to consciously think about it. This is the social pragmatic language layer of neurotypical communication. It has unspoken rules, conventions, and expectations. Because of these hidden, subconscious layers, much miscommunication and frustration can result between autistic and neurotypical individuals. These miscommunications can be better understood simply by noticing that they exist. We can then build a bridge to each other's different ways of thinking. In Nest's therapeutic intervention, SDI, this bridge is constructed with a commitment to mutual perspective-taking, flexible communication tools, and a willingness to construct a *new, cooperative social language*.

Nowhere is this bridge needed more than in the school environment. After all, learning from adults and with peers requires a shared engagement in the world. Consider the Individuals with Disabilities Education Improvement Act (IDEA 2004). The law requires special education programs to ensure access to the general curriculum and to help students meet the same educational standards as other students in their school. A large part of what autistic students need in order to participate in the curriculum is working with their peers. Engagement with peers is an essential part of learning for all students in classrooms. "Teachers use peer conversations as an opportunity to discuss curriculum topics, engage learners, and build a classroom community" (Lloyd, Kolodziej, and Brashears 2016). As a result, students with autism who have difficulty initiating communication with, and responding to, their peers may be considerably disadvantaged in the classroom setting" (Sutton 2019). Sallie Nowell's study on social communication interventions (2019) reported that "social communication deficits have been shown to negatively affect academic performance ... and affect friendship and employment outcomes in adulthood." The development of social communication is therefore a critical part of any academic program for autistic children. Social communication support is crucial in the school environment, and cannot be just a pull-out service but must be integrated into the whole school environment.

There is a further need. The academic and testing expectations in relation to autistic students' diverse ways of thinking are often ill-matched. In New York City, the NYS Next Generation Learning Standards were not written with autistic students' communication needs in mind. In Nest, we consider how the underlying social challenges of autism can complicate a full understanding of the language, communication, and social skills embedded in the NYS Next Generation Learning Standards. In addition to Nest's classroom structure, SDI provides this differentiated support and directly links the therapeutic work to academic learning.

Central to this school-based model is the recognition that therapeutic interventions must address these unique social communication needs of autistic students. Deficits in social communication and social interaction across multiple contexts are defining criteria of an autism diagnosis, as named in the *Diagnostic and Statistical Manual of Mental Disorders* (DSM) edition V (American Psychiatric Association 2013). In SDI, we consider these criteria and shift the deficit-based thinking to Dr. Melanie Heyworth's neurodiversity-affirming lens as defined in *A Manifesto for Allies Adopting an Acceptance Approach to Autism* (Heyworth 2019). She focuses on certain characteristic qualities of autism, including differences in how autistic individuals do the following:

- Communicate, with many classed as non-traditional communicators
- Experience and display emotions
- Interact with others
- Form and define friendships and relationships
- Engage in areas of passion or expertise
- Innovate, imagine, and play
- See patterns and connections
- Perceive or sense the world around them

Through this lens, we provide accommodations to students with a more proactive and strength-based approach. This supports building awareness and competence over remediation and forming rote skills.

SDI's History

In the Nest program's 2003 pilot year, no one intervention existed with the Nest's specific variables in mind. However, with promising practices and evidence-based support evolving in the field of autism, it was an exciting time to build a therapeutic model and adapt it to a school setting. We drew from developmental and pragmatic language therapies, followed the latest research, considered the inclusive classroom environment, and began learning as a team to "speak autism."

With the underlying challenges of autism relevant to being a fully included learner in mind, a developmental therapeutic model evolved, eventually coined Social Development Intervention (SDI). It focused on building social pragmatic awareness and facilitating engagement in the school setting for inclusive learning. As our students grew, so did our model. A fundamental shift began in 2009 as SDI's developmental foundation and growing social cognitive work became directly informed by the experience of autistic adults and the expansion of the model into middle and high schools.

In 2019, after fourteen years of drawing on the experiences of multiple schools and after learning to listen to both autistic self-advocates and directly to our students, we rolled out an evolved and expanded therapy: SDI 2.0. We embraced the authentic and messy nature of communication, allowing it to guide our therapy. We examined how generational, cultural, racial, religious, gender expression, and ability differences impact how allistic adults and practitioners perceive "successful interactions." Then we recalibrated to what positive interactions actually are for five- to eleven-year-olds. We put all of our support through the filter of The Five A's, created by a Nest Support Project team member, Jules Csillag, with Susan Ehlerman in 2019, asking ourselves, "Is my facilitation Authentic? Accurate? Affirming? Absolutely Necessary? and Accessible?" Through these questions, we kept what worked, expanded upon it, and added new frameworks.

SDI's Foundational Tenets

Relationship-Based

The founders of Nest steered us in the direction of building a relational therapy from day one, and this, rather than teaching social skills, remains essential to SDI 2.0. After all, if Nest's language therapy intends to support students in learning together in the classroom, we need to give them a foundation for interacting and communicating with one another. SDI was influenced by other relationship-based models such as Steven Gutstein's RDI (2000), Stanley Greenspan's Floortime (2006) and The Hanen Centre program (see Sussman reference). With the ultimate goal of supporting students' access to the curriculum and generalization into the full school environment, we adapted relational approaches influenced by these interventions for our language-based therapy.

Developmental Social Pragmatics (DSP)

Developmental social pragmatics has also remained foundational to SDI. DSP interventions have much overlap with relationship-based therapies yet are rooted in language development and focus on building social engagement, communicative intent, and the flexible use of symbols within meaningful contexts (Gerber 2003). The DSP considers communication differences in autism by merging the scientific study of typical language development with findings concerning autistic social communication (Rogers 2006). It recognizes that autistic children do not build language from early motivators such as connections made through joint attention or gestures to affect one's environment and people. We work from these differences in development to do the following:

1. Provide opportunities for engagement that highlight communication building blocks in a naturally occurring context.
2. Provide a rich social language environment to put the social world on student's radar.
3. Recognize differences in development, thinking, and communication rather than focusing on deficits.
4. Identify communication strengths as a springboard for taking on communication challenges and utilizing one's intrinsic competence.
5. Build awareness of neurotypical social communication and expectations as students become cognitively ready to "think through the social world."
6. Give students practice in authentic interactions while eliminating the expectation that they will communicate as their neurotypical peers do.
7. Build a foundation that balances awareness of social expectations with knowing one's own communication preferences and needs.

Because speech and language therapy is already integrated into public schools, DSP was possible and could be a strong therapeutic support to autistic students. In more recent years, studies have shown consistent empirical support for the effectiveness of DSP interventions to "positively impact children's foundational social communication capacities, such as attention, focusing on faces, joint attention, initiation, and reciprocity" (Binns and Cardy 2019).

By marrying DSP and relationship-based theories, SDI moved beyond teaching rote social skills and communication rules to what drives interaction and experience sharing with others. Recognizing that language development will vary for autistic students, the SLP, in collaboration with teachers, occupational therapists, guidance counselors, and families, can support engagement, awareness, social cognition, and, ultimately, each student's ability to advocate for their own communication needs and desires.

Generalization

A commitment to generalization was, is, and always will be essential to SDI's integration into the full Nest Model. Through case conferencing, ongoing collaboration around relevant social communication concepts and strategies, and the SLP's turn-keying of SDI information at team meetings, the model had committed to an "all hands on deck" approach to social supports. Rather than a pull-out model of therapy, classroom teachers actively participate in SDI sessions and are the bridge to bringing differentiated supports from the therapy room back to the classroom.

Self-Determination: SDI's Theory of Motivation

Drawing from Ryan and Deci's seminal article on self-determination (2000), we believed that if students were going to actively engage in learning with their peers, they needed to be intrinsically motivated to do so. Learning a social "skill" may or may not be motivating and, similarly, may or may not be relevant in varying contexts. Additionally, and this was pivotal in the work, we understood from this concept that students with a different neurology than their neurotypical peers were not going to subconsciously learn to "think like a neurotypical" and then authentically interact like one, nor should that be the goal. Therefore, self-determination theory became SDI's "theory of motivation." Additionally, we saw the importance of beginning to build this foundation in elementary school for the adolescent work of self-advocacy, which leads to SDI's ultimate goal: interdependence.

With this thinking, we further capitalized on strengths and interests to motivate communication. We believe that students have interests they want to share (autonomy), can build on these interests, and have strengths in social communication that are often overlooked (competence). If, when exploring one's social awareness, the student has little choice about the content of an interaction, if they are told what information to share and how to share it, and if they have no opportunity to share with their peers what excites them (relatedness), they will be hard pressed to be motivated to interact, not to mention generalize interaction to the classroom and beyond.

What Was Added and Evolved in SDI 2.0

Because the field of autism is rapidly evolving, with the internet giving us greater access to autistic advocates and with valuable research that includes autistic guidance and perspectives, the following principles were added to the SDI model. We remain committed to continually growing and expanding SDI as we learn more in the field and from the experts.

SDI's THEORETICAL FOUNDATION 2.0

Like many interventions, SDI started with the once-standard theories around autism to better understand our student's thinking: theory of mind, central coherence, and executive functioning. These theories can explain autistic communication, but it is from a "breakdown in neurotypical communication" perspective. **Double empathy theory** then solidly replaced theory of mind, which put the onus of responsibility on the autistic partner to do all of the perspective-taking or to "think about what someone else is thinking." Support for executive functioning remains essential in Nest, and the model directly supports this work in the classroom. While there is a crossover to social language, we no longer see it as foundational to our therapeutic work. SDI's focus on students ultimately being self-determined in their communication rather than needing to organize it, meant **self-determination theory** (explained in "SDI Foundational Tenets") would remain one of the primary theories of SDI. **Context sensitivity** expands on our original thinking around central coherence by also considering the *use* of context to make meaning in social situations.

Context

In his 2012 book *Autism as Context Blindness*, Peter Vermeulen, a Belgian psychologist and educator, expanded and modified the concept of central coherence to suggest that autistic people have a reduced ability to use context spontaneously when giving meaning to vague, ambiguous, and abstract stimuli. The autistic brain can see context but may not use it to inform communication. Vermeulen's work led to another shift in Nest's social support. It explained the different social language processing of autistics and neurotypicals (stimulus-driven instead of context-driven) and deepened our understanding of autistic thinking.

It became clear that often, the autistic students we worked with were not subconsciously altering their language processing and expression to match the context. With this awareness, we could better understand where social misunderstandings might originate and start to build social concepts with the added knowledge that they would change based on the context. In SDI language, anytime we consider a standard rule, we add: "it depends," which is our language around context shifts.

> **I used to blame myself for every miscommunication. After all, I was the one who couldn't figure things out as easily as others. Now, I embrace my neurotype & Autistic culture. Miscommunication is a two-way street.**
>
> \- Lauren Melissa Elizey

FIGURE 9.1: Elizey, L. M. (n.d.). Autistic Care: Communication Differences. Autinelle Instagram. Retrieved June 3, 2024, from https://www.instagram.com/p/CpYE1cduAtX/?img_index=10

Double Empathy

Our early framework of the Middleground™ (explained later in the implementation section of this chapter) is now supported by Damian Milton's theory on the double empathy problem (2012). Specific to its relevance in SDI, an interaction defined by only one neurotype's social rules is imbalanced, lacks awareness, and causes endless confusion between those of different neurotypes. Teaching autistic students to communicate like neurotypicals and putting all of the communication work on autistics to change is not reciprocal communication. The idea that autistic people are the only ones who struggle to take the perspective of those with a different neurology is false. And once you know this, you can't unknow it. This theory not only supports the Middleground™ but demands that we as allistic educators and therapists build awareness around our own challenges in taking the perspective of autistics. This can and should cause a dramatic shift in communication therapy. Rather than expecting autistic students to memorize rules, imitate interactions, or mask and perform as neurotypicals, this theory suggests that a new way to communicate is necessary. This is the type of communication that SDI fully embraces.

CHAPTER 9

Elementary SDI Is a Social Playground

People question if this supported two-way communication framework, which asks for both parties to shift how they interact, is possible outside the walls of a Nest school where the structure is built into the setting. After all, we can't train all humans to communicate this way. The answer is that school itself is rarely an exact replica of the outside world. It is practice. It is an environment that builds the skills that go *into* life. Very little that children do outside of school has the same demands or logistics, or offers the same support as the educational environment. Instead, we are creating a world to which the student can best correspond, so they can then practice and build awareness and competence. They are learning, practicing, and "flexing" various skills that they can take with them. Elementary school is a rich time of growth when we create what we call a "social playground." Here students can try on, mess up, explore, choose, opt out, enjoy, and find their social communication preferences, challenges, and strengths, and experience them as they change over time. SDI (language, concepts, supports) builds self-awareness around communication, which supports self-regulation and ultimately allows students to invite others into their communication and/or advocate around their needs and desires.

SDI Implementation: Frameworks, Strategies, and Tools

Implementing SDI therapy with fidelity across different schools in vastly different NYC neighborhoods is a "good problem." It has forced us to grow, be flexible, find core tenets and supporting research, listen to the lived experience of autistic adults, and recognize that "this too will change." In SDI, we wanted practitioners to have a container for a different way of supporting autistic students. However, even the most thoughtful strategies and supports can be used to control behavior rather than build interconnectedness. So it became clear early on that teams would need to do a good deal of perspective-taking work and self-reflection to support authentic communication. They would need ways to deliver the intervention and, on an ongoing basis, check their work around being neurodiversity-affirming as well as culturally sensitive. The following are frameworks, tools, and strategies essential to delivering SDI.

Collaboration

While we focus on building social communication in SDI therapeutic sessions, it is also the vehicle for social supports throughout the school day. Interdisciplinary collaboration, particularly between school speech-language pathologists and classroom teachers, is essential to both a comprehensive implementation of SDI and holistic support of Nest students.

To this end, the SLP does ongoing diagnostic therapy to write goals and follow progress, which is then shared at Nest team meetings. Planning sessions tailored to each group's needs, the SLP collaborates with staff on relevant social concepts and runs the SDI groups *with* classroom teachers. In SDI sessions, the SLP creates a language-rich environment to spark social interactions and investigate social concepts which can then be carried over into classrooms.

The classroom teachers, however, are the key to the generalization of SDI and social supports. They are the bridge for Nest students to take this social awareness back and forth between therapy and the classroom. Teachers provide essential classroom information to inform pre-session planning with the SLP, making the therapeutic work relevant to each student. They also take the language and strategies from sessions back to the classroom, providing ongoing social communication modeling and support.

> **When we talk about "not pathologizing autism," we don't mean "pretending autistic people don't have impairments." But we also don't assume that neurological and behavioral differences are always problems. For example, there's nothing inherently wrong with disliking social activities. Not wanting to socialize is different from wanting to participate and being unable to. Both are possibilities for autistic people. One requires acceptance, the other requires assistance.**
>
> **- Aiyana Bailin**

FIGURE 9.2: Aiyana Bailin June 6, 2019. Clearing Up Some Misconceptions about Neurodiversity, Scientific American Blog Network.

Neurodiversity- and Intersectionality-Affirming Practices

As we learned more from autistic self-advocates like Aiyana Bailin about neurodiversity-affirming practices, we added an ongoing self-reflection piece to our SLP training and seminars, challenging our own biases around what it means to be social. Disparities in access during the COVID-19 lockdown and a nationwide racial reckoning demanded that we intentionally foster our own cultural, generational, (anti) ableist, racial, identity-based, and social humility to fully support our students' best-fit communication. We continue to learn directly from autistic self-advocates to ask ourselves hard questions about our practice and the implementation of SDI. In an ongoing way, we investigate what it means to be an SDI therapist and commit to changing when necessary to be truly neurodiversity-affirming. The following are the agreements we offer therapists at the end of their initial training and throughout our intermediate seminars.

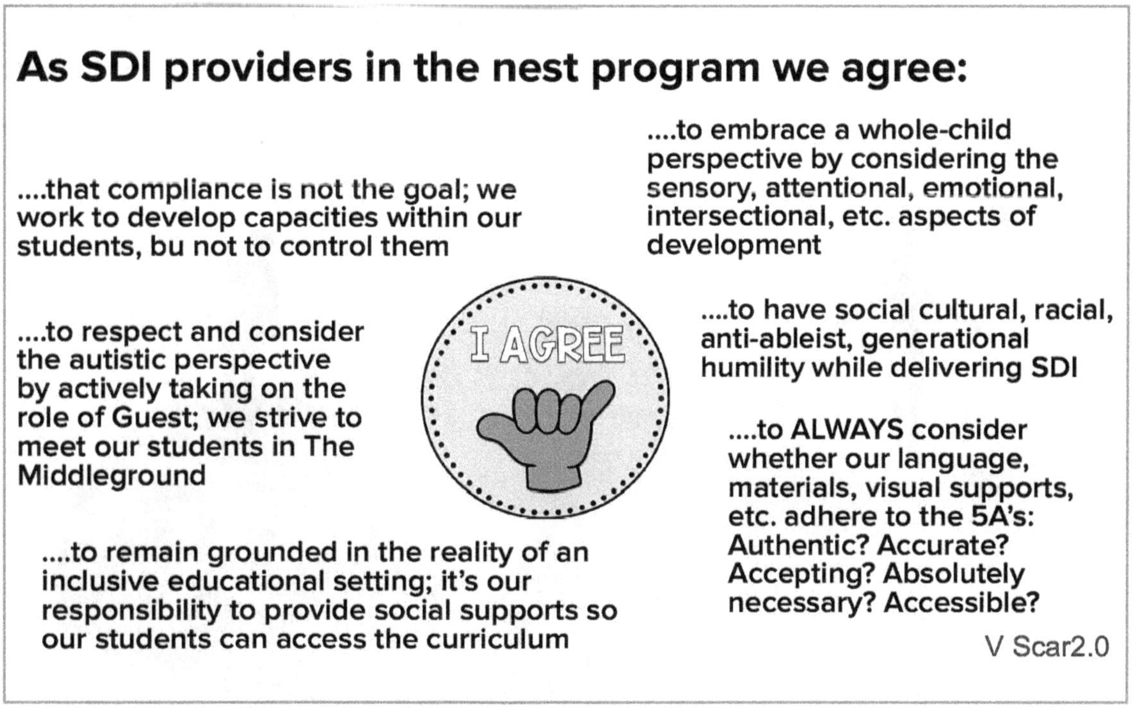

As SDI providers in the nest program we agree:

....that compliance is not the goal; we work to develop capacities within our students, bu not to control them

....to embrace a whole-child perspective by considering the sensory, attentional, emotional, intersectional, etc. aspects of development

....to respect and consider the autistic perspective by actively taking on the role of Guest; we strive to meet our students in The Middleground

I AGREE

....to have social cultural, racial, anti-ableist, generational humility while delivering SDI

....to ALWAYS consider whether our language, materials, visual supports, etc. adhere to the 5A's: Authentic? Accurate? Accepting? Absolutely necessary? Accessible?

....to remain grounded in the reality of an inclusive educational setting; it's our responsibility to provide social supports so our students can access the curriculum

V Scar2.0

FIGURE 9.3. Nest SDI Agreements

Nest SLP's explore Virginia Scar's "SDI Agreements" once they receive their initial training. This requires a paradigm shift in the therapist's thinking in order to support social communication within the Nest Model.

The Middleground

After the first six years of learning and listening to advocates, we shifted our implementation to a framework that lies at SDI's foundation: **The Middleground**™ (Ehlerman). An exchange with autistic advocate John Scott Holman sparked the need for a therapeutic paradigm shift when he shared the following: "We are autistic. We are not occasionally autistic, we are always autistic. When we seem to be particularly level-headed, caring, understanding, and socially poised, it is only because we are trying very, very hard. Social adaptation is not exclusively our responsibility. All of us must work together to better understand one another." Agreeing with this statement was not enough. We needed an active way to engage in and invite reciprocity.

The Middleground encourages an awareness of both neurotypical and autistic communication styles. The goal is to teach autistic students how social interactions work for neurotypicals *and* to build students' awareness of how interactions work best for them. Starting from this place of knowing, we can generate a new and more productive way of communicating.

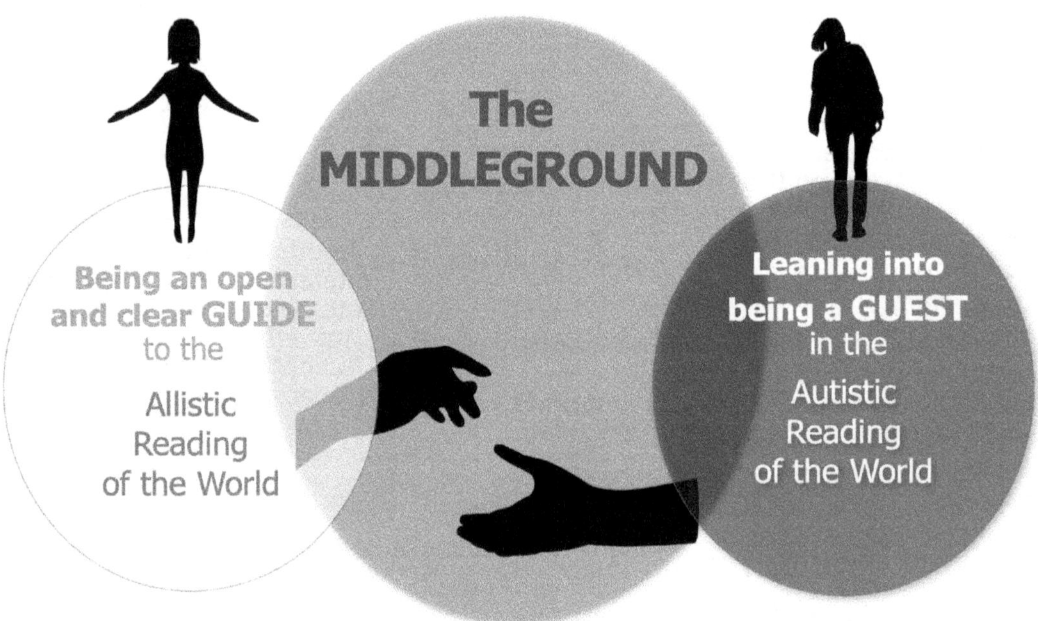

FIGURE 9.4. The Middleground™ framework

CHAPTER 9

The Middleground™ framework arose from an understanding that special education and pragmatic language therapy traditionally support students, albeit with good intention, in a one-directional way: "Don't worry, I know how to do this, and I will teach you." The intention is to help students learn a social skill and/or internalize a type of thinking, yet it is often heavily based on neurotypical communication. Sometimes, we can encourage a student into our way of thinking, but one's neurology wins out: a rote skill, one that rarely succeeds in multiple contexts, is often counter to an autistic student's natural communication style, and can require continuous extrinsic motivators, is learned. For example, a common rote skill is teaching a student to take one to three conversational turns. This structure might work in a small number of contexts but would not apply to many, such as classroom lessons, when listening to a friend's story, or when sharing a non-verbal reaction with a classmate. Additionally, counting turns and performing the skill can squelch any authentic interaction that may have naturally arisen. To offer a more balanced communication space, adults take on two roles when inviting students into the Middleground: Guide and Guest.

A **Guide** not only knows the language and customs of their culture (in this case, the "social world") but also recognizes what a visitor (the student) does not easily see or read. In this way, the guide brings their subconscious knowledge of social constructs, abstract language, and facial expressions to the surface and translates it for the student. When guiding, we first recognize that we read social language intuitively and do not have to stop and think about it. However, our students need time to think and focus on this communication element. Guides make the subconscious conscious to put the social world on our students' radars.

Alternately, a **Guest** listens closely, follows the other's lead, and asks questions if uncertain. When visiting someone's home for the first time, we do not apply our own set of rules but adjust and follow our host's way of engaging with their world. "Guesting," in two-way communication, is mindfully considering the perspective of the student and opening up to their way of interacting. The adult moves between these two roles to meet each student in the balanced space of the Middleground.

The 8 Underlying Social Challenges

For teams to better understand our Nest students' communication difficulties, we needed a comprehensive framework that considered the demands of group learning. We began in 2003 by considering the deficits that impacted students' interactions. As we grew away from deficit-based thinking and looked more deeply at autistic students' perspectives, our Eight Underlying Social Challenges when communicating with neurotypicals solidified. This is the lens through which we view each student's communication profiles, which in turn guides the goals, planning, and implementation of an SDI session.

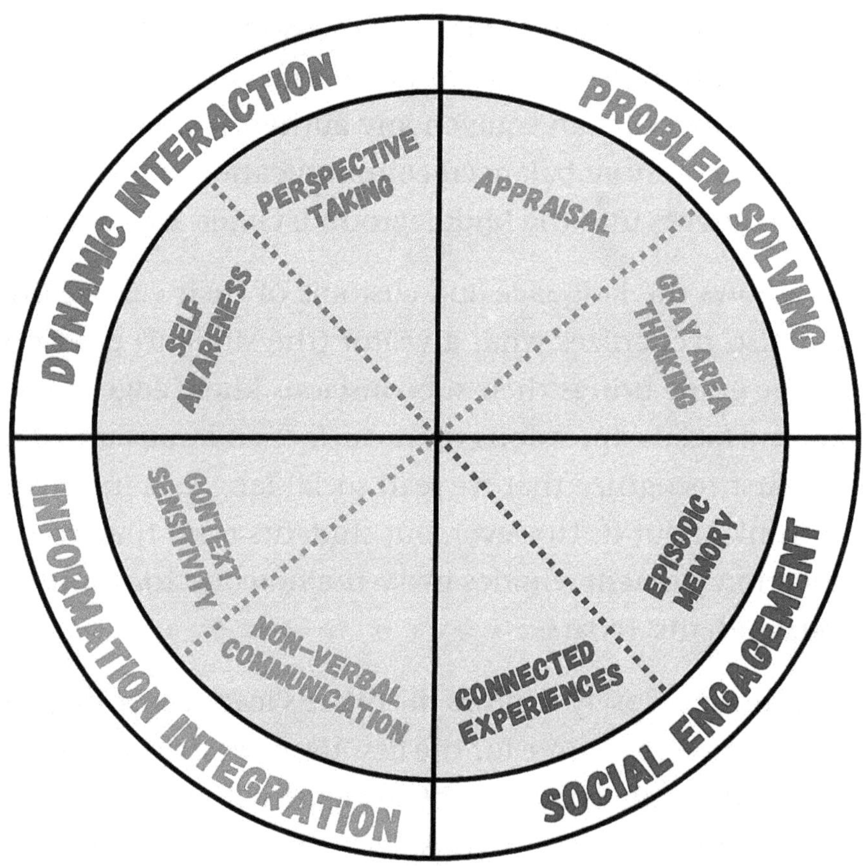

FIGURE 9.5. SDI's Underlying Social Challenges Framework

The challenges are categorized into four focus areas or "quads." These guide practitioners in developing a therapeutic "best-fit" way for students to access and engage in the school environment. The quads also provide Nest teams with a shared map to decipher present social functioning, a guide to enriching communication, and a direction for identifying relevant social supports. They are broken down as follows:

Social Engagement is involvement with and connection to others during a communicative exchange. To build this, we encourage, allow, notice, highlight, and refer back to unique moments of connection.

Dynamic Interaction involves staying regulated during emotional shifts, when changing activity, and when given novel information within a communicative exchange. Therapeutically, this involves building an awareness of one's self as a communicator and fostering the ability to recognize that others have perspectives that can be used to inform an interaction.

Problem-Solving is finding solutions to communication breakdowns in order to engage in shared moments. Interactions can be complicated since these moments include varying perspectives and emotional responses. At the elementary level, students are given practice with pausing and "sizing up" social situations, which are rarely black-and-white and call for "thinking in the gray."

Information integration is processing relevant, constantly changing communicative stimuli and incorporating them into interactions. At the elementary developmental stages, SDI is building a sensitivity to and offering practice with noticing nonverbal and contextual cues.

SDI Sessions

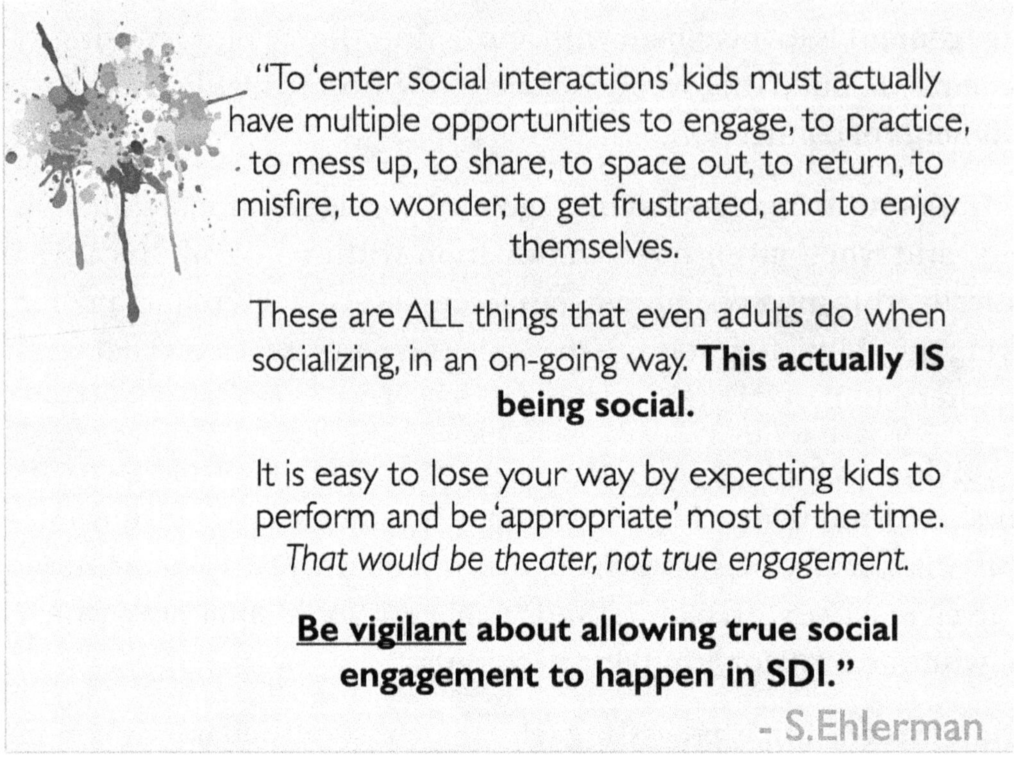

"To 'enter social interactions' kids must actually have multiple opportunities to engage, to practice, to mess up, to share, to space out, to return, to misfire, to wonder, to get frustrated, and to enjoy themselves.

These are ALL things that even adults do when socializing, in an on-going way. **This actually IS being social.**

It is easy to lose your way by expecting kids to perform and be 'appropriate' most of the time. *That would be theater, not true engagement.*

Be vigilant about allowing true social engagement to happen in SDI."

- S.Ehlerman

FIGURE 9.6. Social engagement

Social Engagement and Social Cognitive Balance

As a developmental therapy, SDI sessions balance social engagement and social cognitive work, calibrated loosely by grades and, more specifically, to the developmental readiness of each student. We support bottom-up processing by facilitating social engagement activities where students experience interactions in real time. Students can take these experiences and relate them to future social moments. We employ top-down processing with our social-cognitive work by utilizing prior knowledge of experiences to think through social interactions. This thinking can then inform future experiences. Whether an activity is designed for experience sharing, thinking through information, or both, all activities connect to the relevant social contexts. A commitment to noting this changing social information keeps SDI concepts from being acontextual and, therefore, inflexible from one environment to the next.

ELEMENTARY SDI SESSION: Providing a Structure That Encourages Authentic Interactions (part 1)

With the lights off, four children stand at the Social Explorers Club door with their teachers. "When the sun comes up we'll be able to see the path through the woods in the park more clearly, explorers," observes Jamie, their teacher. Jayden turns on the light and Sam runs to the front saying, "I'll lead the way. Come on, stay connected everyone." Kylie stays at the door and Caitlin says she wants to lead the way to the fountain (bucket of water in the middle of the rug). After Sam reminds everyone that she is already the leader, the teacher notes that that is true. "Sam is assigned leader and we can keep it that way. However, it would be okay with me if there are two leaders helping the group get through the trees (chairs places around the room)." "Hm. I'm the leader. Annnd ..." sighs Sam, "I'm saying you can be my partner leader, Caaaaiitlin." Jayden falls in line and the teacher invites Kylie to move with the team to get to the center of the park together. Jayden sings, "Oh yeah! Team work makes the dream work!" and Sam joins in, loudly directing the song at Kylie. Kylie responds by walking to the fountain in front of everyone. Sam furrows her eyebrows and looks at Jamie who says, "Ah, Kylie went on his own. He changed his plan. Can you still get the rest of us to the center of the park?" Stomping a bit, Sam runs with everyone to the rug to sit around the fountain. Carina, the SLP, is already there and starts the Welcome Social Explorers campfire song. When it is over, she looks to the schedule, which has a boat next to each item and says, "Let's keep the boats afloat today, team. Lots of boats to use! I remember what kept the boats floating yesterday ..." She reminds them of something each student used in the last session that helped to keep the group together and work as a team.

FIGURE 9.7. SDI Session Part 1

The vignette in Figure 9.6 illustrates a play-based activity that offers enough structure to encourage natural engagement. Students are familiar with this type of activity, they take on roles, and when necessary, they think through solutions. Therapeutically, SDI defines *social engagement activities* as authentic interactions experienced live and in the moment. It is actually being in the experience rather than reflecting on it; this is the "doing" component of SDI. In kindergarten through second grade, this involves play, immersing students in a rich social language, building a bank of positive social experiences and memories, and capitalizing on authentic moments. In kindergarten through second or third grade, social engagement is a large part of a session. SDI engagement activities in third to fifth grades continue this "social playground" work while more directly building on social connectedness, exploring shared interests, and utilizing self-identified roles in group games. In upper elementary, there is a growing focus on actually discussing communication through social cognitive work, the "thinking" component in SDI, in order to prepare students for the changes in adolescent social communication.

Finally, we must honor the taxing nature of social interactions and build awareness that taking space is a necessary part of communication. Therefore, within this calibration, there is a third SDI component that is woven throughout: "space and time" for regulating and recharging. Were we to focus on just one of these—the doing (engagement piece), or the thinking (social-cognitive work), or on supporting regulation (space and time), the therapy would have value. However, creating sessions that provide all three types of therapy is SDI.

ELEMENTARY SDI SESSION: Providing a Structure That Encourages Authentic Interactions (part 2)

The kindergarten team is going on a scavenger hunt for dinner supplies. Carina, the SLP, guides the assigning of roles for this group to encourage teamwork. Carina talks through this planning by brainstorming with the students. She models her thinking about what is needed to collaborate and uses some declarative language to invite ideas.

Carina begins, "Someone will need to read this map to help us find (Jayden jumps up) ... yes, Jayden! Since you are a map expert, the park ranger is a good job for you. You can direct the team where to go. Since it is getting dark soon, there needs to be someone guiding the group with this flashlight ... (Sam says, "me!" And Kylie raises his thumb.) Okay, Sam—you did a nice job sharing the leader job when we came to the fountain. You can hold the flashlight and lead the group on our hunt. Kylie, there are some post-its to mark our way so we can find our way back and we also really need someone who can carry the basket to collect the food. I remember that you helped Sumi with her backpack yesterday; you could carry the basket for all of us while we collect the food." (His head in hands and eyes diverted, Kylie puts one hand out for the basket, and then the other out for the post-its.) "Oops ... someone is missing" notes Carina. (Caitlin is turned away and reading a book.) Kylie rolls hi says and says, "Caitlin, take the basket, would you!" She takes it while also carrying the book. "Okay—it's up to you team. Jayden, the map will tell you where to find the food. Sam has the light to guide us, and Kylie can make sure we know how to get back. Once you find the food, Caitlin has a place to hold it all. Ok! You've got what you need to work together, find dinner, and bring it back to the fountain. I'm here if you need me."

FIGURE 9.8. SDI Session Part 2

SDI Strategies

The vehicles to deliver a neurodiversity-affirming therapy with fidelity are the SDI strategies, of which there are a core fifteen. Strategies are introduced in therapy sessions and then bridged into the classrooms. Following are five of the most common SDI strategies.

- **Declarative Language:** stating out loud (declaring) what one knows or thinks in the form of a comment. This is sharing your thinking and does not require a verbal response. It invites experience sharing and provides an ideal social framework for later interactions.
- **Directive Language:** language used for the purpose of causing (or preventing) overt action or confusion. Commands and questions are forms of directive language. We *guide* with this language and use it to be concrete and clear when the context calls for it.
- **Wait Time:** waiting for an intentional amount of time after asking a question or making a verbal or nonverbal comment so that a student or students can

The Data Support It!

Dr. Kristie Patten

In our National Science Foundation project (NSF#1614436) entitled IDEAS, Inventing, Designing and Engineering with Autistic Students, interest-based maker clubs let students build and create with their interests and passions and socially, be their authentic selves. It is a high-functioning environment that is core to the Nest philosophy. In strengths-based focused research, Chen et al. (2021) observed social behaviors and interactions between autistic and nonautistic middle school students, but through a double empathy theory lens posited by autistic researcher Damian Milton. Milton's (2012) "double empathy problem" suggests that when people with very different experiences of the world interact with one another, they struggle to empathize with each other. In most Nest formal and informal environments, because of the model of four to five autistic students in each class, there are opportunities not only for inclusive cross-neurotype interaction but much more within-neurotype interaction, central to the Nest Model. Chen et al. (2021) confirmed that mutual understanding and better interactions were seen among youth within rather than across neurotypes. In other words, autistic-to-autistic social interaction did not have "autistic social deficits." This suggests that autistic social difficulties may result from differences in the social expectations and profiles between autistic and nonautistic youth. Interventions, then, to support peer engagement among autistic youth should focus on facilitating mutual understanding across neurotypes and promoting a culture of openness to non-normative social styles versus an overfocus on the autistic social deficits (Patten 2022). This is what the Nest program does on a daily basis, and that is what has been qualitatively different and transformative.

gather their thoughts before responding, because processing social information takes time.

- **Providing Observations:** clear, short, simple descriptions of what you can see, hear, or touch. This is a concrete, neutral comment free of evaluation, judgment, analysis, or interpretation.
- **Using SDI Language:** concepts and vocabulary that highlight otherwise invisible or subconscious social moments. The team uses this language to put such moments on students' radar and "flex" these concepts across contexts.

Seeing SDI in the hands of hundreds of therapists and teachers over twenty years has taught us that how these strategies are used really matters! So we have multiple ways for practitioners to check and optimize this part of their practice. Here are two:

1. The 5 A's: Constructed by our Nest colleague Jules Csillag as we updated to SDI 2.0. The 5 A's are essential for therapists to check their own implementation of SDI. They are a self-reflection structure for therapists to ask themselves if their work is: Authentic? Accurate? Affirming? Absolutely Necessary? Accessible?

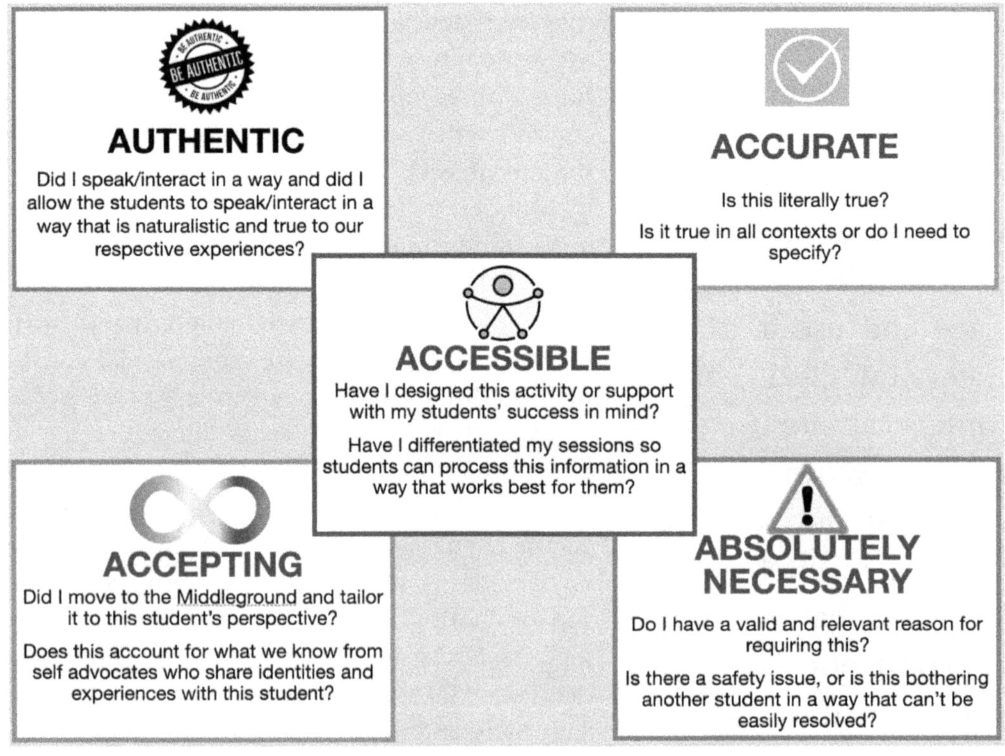

FIGURE 9.9. The 5 A's

2. Trapdoors: All strategies can be used in a way they were not intended, and the "trapdoor" reflection on delivery helps assess that. If a strategy is used to promote rote skills, change behavior with judgment, or control, then it is not an SDI strategy. If, however, it is used to encourage engagement and support challenges neutrally and supportively with validation and belief, then it *is* SDI.

   Consider the strategy of using SDI language and concepts in the term "brain match!" This is a way to simply highlight a moment of connection (e.g., "Ahh, brain match! You both thought to hide the Pokémon rather than keep it in the box. Smart.") The trapdoors are overusing the term so it loses its meaning, keeping it rigid and not using this language in varying contexts such as only in the therapy room, over time never moving to more naturalistic uses such as, "I was thinking the same thing," or, "Two great minds work as one!" or controlling behavior, for example: "You two are not connecting. You need to find a brain match." All SDI strategies have trapdoors, and with an awareness of them, you can avoid them and encourage true connection.

Conclusion

SDI was designed to support Nest students in building their social communication so that they could, first and foremost, dynamically engage with their peers in learning. As the model grew, SDI 2.0's ultimate goal in the elementary years expanded to building a foundation in social language that would allow students to one day advocate for their own communication needs and preferences in order to reach interdependence.

Our influences have been the program's growth throughout New York City, progress in autism research, and direct guidance from autistic advocates and professionals. Like an SDI session, the therapy itself is built to be responsive, flexible, and authentic in its delivery. The intervention has been specifically tailored to fluidly meld and change based on each student's needs and growth over time. This design allows for ongoing staff reflection on the work and its delivery, so that we continue to evolve to a day where SDI 3.0 is possible. For now, we relish the joy and growth that is possible for Nest students who have so much to offer on the social playground of school and in the world around them.

CHAPTER 10

A Positive and Proactive Approach

Katie Kirkman

A positive and proactive approach is one of our philosophical foundations as we recognize that meeting students where they are and recognizing their strengths is the best way to ensure they thrive in our learning spaces. Based on this, in the Nest program, behavior is addressed in a holistic manner that takes into account the individual neurotype and identity of each child. Nest classrooms focus on implementing proactive supports and encourage adaptive problem-solving alongside the development of regulation and self-advocacy as opposed to emphasizing compliance-based responses. Nest teams partner with students to cultivate a classroom culture and norms where students feel they belong and where students and teachers can work collaboratively when challenges inevitably come up.

Nest's Evolving Approach

When Nest was originally conceptualized, the strongest and most evidence-based classroom practices centered around concepts taken from applied behavior analysis (ABA) literature. Positive behavior supports (PBS) is one such methodology that was becoming more and more popular in schools in an effort to shift away from consequences and focus on the use of positive and proactive strategies. Thus, while Nest was never an ABA-based program, in the beginning, the Nest Model focused on whole-class PBS systems for motivation and, when challenges arose, approached students' behavior from an assessment and data-driven perspective in order to implement individualized behavior plans to encourage behavior change. While some of this original practice can still be found in our model, things have evolved. After listening to the voices of autistic advocates, it was loud and clear that a more neurodivergence-inclusive lens was warranted, as well as a focus on understanding and supporting the student's underlying needs.

Based on feedback from the lived experiences of autistics and other experts in the field, we deepened our understanding of neurodiversity-affirming practice and developed a more robust approach to challenges that arose in Nest schools.

In a 2017 report, authored by Finn Gardiner and put out by the ASAN (Autistic Self Advocacy Network), a group of autistic self-advocates presented some personal perspectives and guidelines on behavioral interventions for people with developmental disabilities. That report outlined the basic values they considered important in behavioral treatment, including, "Promoting Positive Outcomes and Preventing Harm, Protecting Autonomy, Being Inclusive (including: promotion of self-advocacy skills, providing accessibility, and social inclusion), Being Trauma-Sensitive, Promoting Cultural Competency."

There was an overall call for a more dynamic and less rigid lens: care over compliance. Nest took these values into consideration when evolving our behavioral framework. It was extremely beneficial to have such a resource that specifically looked at behavior therapy, and the values cited by this report align well with the values on which the program was built and with the self-determination theory framework that can be seen throughout our model.

Self-Determination Theory and Belonging

The current Nest Model is deeply rooted in self-determination theory (see chapter 4), which asserts that autistic students should have access to a personally meaningful education that supports their development of self-advocacy and sense of belonging in school spaces. "We need to be allowed to exist and embrace our autistic identity instead of being treated like we are broken or less than," autistic advocate Zoe Williams so beautifully captures the concept of belonging. The Nest classroom is intended to be a space where autistic children can thrive as their authentic autistic selves. Thus, the whole classroom needs to be built as accessible and accepting first, with individual support as needed. Nest practitioners are trained not to see certain behaviors as interfering as much as communicating a need, and are there to help guide the student toward functional methods of self-advocacy. In the Nest program, behavior is addressed in a holistic manner. Part of the proactive framework includes whole-class supports that are connected to the autistic neurotype. As was described in previous chapters, the classroom's sensory environment is carefully considered, and instruction is differentiated based on the student's needs. As such, the Nest classroom is proactively set up with routines, structures, and resources to support regulation and engagement and mitigate potential environmental triggers by implementing supports such as visuals, agendas, timers, priming, and break areas. Additionally, to foster autonomy, competence, and relatedness, Nest educators utilize other preventative measures, including the following:

- Teachers use clear language to support understanding of context and avoid confusion and misinterpretation.
- Teachers use classroom routines to support transitions, including priming and providing clarity about when it is time to move from one activity to another and how to do it.
- Students are provided with access to their interests and passions throughout the day because autistic students learn better, are less anxious, feel more regulated, and encounter fewer challenging situations when that is done.
- Students' strengths and interests are considered when planning learning activities to increase student competence and lead to greater success and motivation. Interests and passions are incorporated non-contingently throughout the day.
- Teachers provide flexibility in their expectations to support students who may have difficulty moving on from an activity, e.g., countdowns, reminders, and preferred activities.
- Teachers plan ahead to reduce wait time and increase autonomy by providing visuals like "when you are finished" task options and "what to do if you are stuck" strategies. (See example below.)

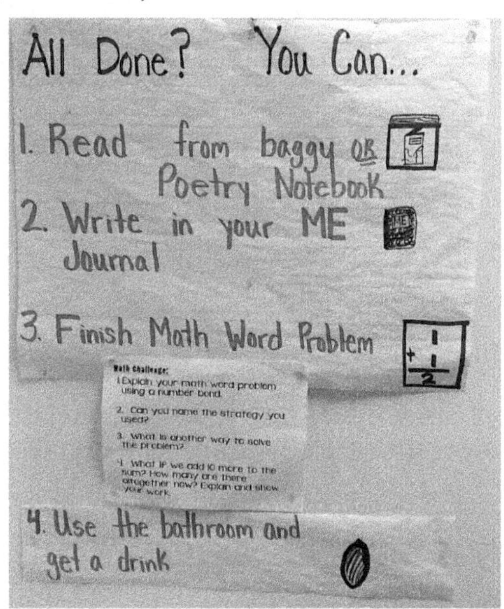

FIGURE 10.1. A classroom support created by F. Falch and I. Nakos, grade 1 teachers at PS 682 in Brooklyn

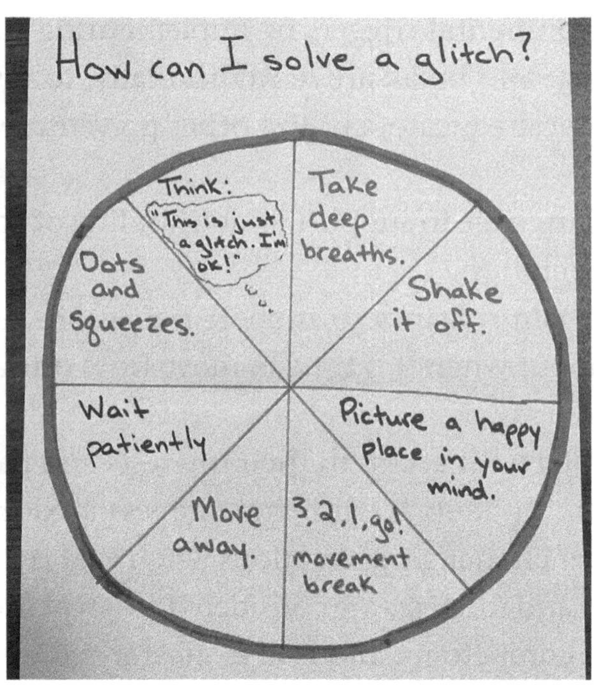

FIGURE 10.2. A classroom support created by J. Loft & J. Goldstein, grade 1 teachers at PS 75 in Manhattan

A sense of belonging and connection are essential for both students and educators in a supportive classroom environment. Autistic students feel more welcome, connected, invested, and motivated in a space where they experience some autonomy and freedom. The true first step in proactively navigating challenging situations is to have learning spaces with support systems of students and adults who care for one another. The Nest classroom is a safe environment where students learn about advocacy alongside interdependence; it is a place where mistakes occur and everyone grows at their own pace. Cultivating this classroom culture takes time, care, and intentionality. Nest teachers recognize that there must be a balance of power between adults and students that fosters self-determination and creates more equitable grounds for navigating challenges. Much of the inspiration behind the Nest's balanced power approach comes from the work of Dr. Carla Shalaby and from the Responsive Classroom Program. Nest educators implement many strategies to make this a reality:

- Teachers and students collaborate to establish the culture and norms of the Nest classroom.
- Lessons and classroom activities include time spent exploring one another's identities and understanding others' perspectives.

- Teachers give time and attention to support students' development of self-awareness, helping them learn about themselves and engage in reflection activities and providing feedback on strengths and how they learn best. (See example below.)

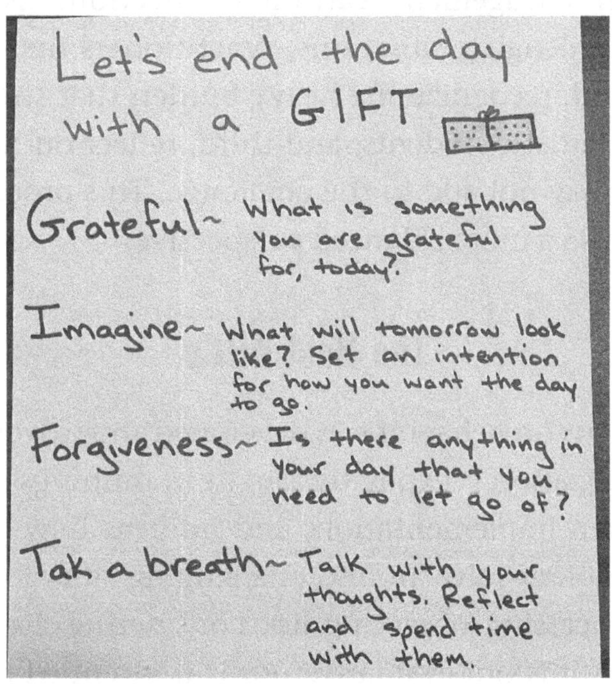

FIGURE 10.3. K. Median & E. Patrakos fourth-grade teachers at PS 165 in Queens end each day with a grounding mindfulness activity: kids come together and share in this moment of connection or, as is known in their class, "A Gift."

Challenging Situations

In the Nest classroom, there is a specific focus on adaptive problem-solving and self-advocating as opposed to an emphasis on compliance. Thus, an approach to behavior that is less about behavior change and more about adaptation in environments and advocacy for one's needs was called for. Similarly, in Nest, instead of talking about a student exhibiting "challenging behaviors," we pause and consider behaviors in the context of "challenging situations." In this way, instead of the onus being on the child to change and exhibit appropriate or desired behavior, the onus is on practitioners to determine how interactions and environmental demands create situations in which students may or may not be able to thrive. To do this, Nest teams ask, "What is the underlying reason for the challenge? Is it the student's unmet need? Is it the practitioner's unmet need? How do the perspectives of each person involved in the situation play a part in the challenge? What aspects of the environment are creating challenges? What is interfering with engagement/learning/connection?" Following this protocol, when encountering challenging situations, practitioners first presume competence in their students; second, recognize the heavy burden that stress and a neurotypical value system place on autistic students; and third, reflect on how their expectations and approach may or may not add to the challenge. This process helps practitioners approach challenges from a more balanced perspective.

The Nest ABCs

In recent years, a Nest lens on behavior was developed and woven into the fabric of the model. This conceptualization is explicitly taught in trainings and professional development, guides program implementation, and informs how educators think about and collaboratively problem-solve around challenging situations. The following outlines the Nest way of processing, observing, and considering challenges we come across in educational settings- it is not evaluative nor is it intended to be used instead of a functional behavior assessment.

All human behavior is an adaptive response to something.
Behavior is an observable action.
Challenging situations involve multiple perspectives.

FIGURE 10.4. Nest's "ABCs of Behavior"

All human behavior is an adaptive response to something *(environment/situation/etc.).*

Behavioral responses differ based on neurotype and identity. Behavioral responses are influenced by signals from the internal nervous system and also may be informed by past experiences. Behavioral responses can contribute to challenging situations. Students have intersecting identities that create unique pasts/responses.

Behavior is an observable action, including what you can see, hear, and count *(i.e., it is specific)*

It's important to recognize that all behavior serves a purpose for the individual and is likely communicating a need. Thus, descriptions of behavior must be objective and neutral, without judgment, evaluation, or assumption. Keep in mind that there is always a reason for a behavior, even if we don't know what that reason is. There is no such thing as non-functional behavior.

Challenging situations involve multiple perspectives.

Rather than looking at challenging behaviors from individual children, we seek to understand challenging situations involving whole contexts and multiple perspectives. It's important to consider: Who is experiencing the challenge, the student or the practitioner? How are different people experiencing the challenging situation—what feelings or concerns are present? What is contributing to the challenge—environment, expectations, etc.? It takes multiple people to work together to solve problems that occur in situations; the onus is never just on the student.

Understanding Behavior

Traditionally, the saying goes, "Behavior is communication," and while that is certainly true, the Nest approach recognizes that we must take time to consider many factors to truly understand what an individual is communicating through their behavior. In her book *Beyond Behaviors*, Mona Delahooke (2019) employs the polyvagal theory (originally introduced in 1994 by Dr. Stephen Porges) to help bring to light the importance of the interaction between the brain and body when considering student behavior. She uses the image of an iceberg to describe how what we see on the surface—the basic form of behavior—is not sufficient in understanding what is really happening during a challenging situation. We have to recognize that there is so much more going on beneath the surface that can help us understand and support our students. Students carry with them their intersectional identities and their past experiences, and as was stated in the Nest ABCs, those things influence behavior. Delahooke's framework pushes us to move away from a mindset where we are trying to figure out, "What is wrong with you?" to one where we instead ask, "What is this child experiencing this moment in body and mind?" (Delahooke, 18).

Traditionally, when working to identify the function of a behavior, we look at the antecedent, what happens right before a behavior, and the setting events and circumstances that may influence the likelihood a behavior occurs. Delahooke provides a new way of viewing the context of a challenge, a way that adds substance to "setting events" and widens the potential impact of "triggers." The developmental iceberg each child figuratively carries with them is composed of biological factors, things like developmental capacities, emotions, predispositions to react to certain sensations, thoughts, memories, and other internal bodily processes (Delahooke, 17). Setting events are often things in a student's environment, but they can also be a part of their social and cultural context.

In Nest, we must consider the autistic experience and acknowledge that what an autistic individual is communicating through their behavior is often misinterpreted. For this reason, Nest behavior courses use the concept of the "iceberg" as a way to examine the form of behavior, what we see, to determine the true function. For example, as was discussed in chapter 8, many autistic students have different sensory-processing experiences and needs than typically developing people, which can often feel intense or overwhelming. Oftentimes, autistic reactions to sensory stimuli can be mistaken for challenging behavior. Executive function can also be difficult for autistic students because of the different ways their brains are wired, and thus, they might need to do things differently. Again, these differences in approach are often misconstrued as defiance or noncompliance. Similarly, autistics have a social culture of their own and do not always immediately pick up on the unspoken rules of neurotypical social situations. Thus, double empathy problems occur and can also come across as behavior challenges when they are simply social misunderstandings. A Nest practitioners' approach to their autistic students is one that takes into consideration these basic elements of autistic neurotype.

Let's consider a student example:

Eno is a sixth-grade student with a tremendous amount of energy. He comes to school and greets everyone he passes by shouting a hearty "Hello!" which can be heard throughout the halls. His teachers often have difficulty getting him to transition into their room and get started on the morning routine because he wants to say "hi" to as many people as he can. During classroom transitions, Eno often starts telling jokes to his peers. Joke telling is also one of Eno's main means of connection in the lunchroom and at recess. He often repeats the same kind of joke over and over, even when the other students don't laugh or find it funny. Other students are starting to avoid him or say mean things when he comes to tell a joke. It seems to Eno's teachers that he might be getting these jokes from somewhere/someone online, and he doesn't fully understand them, but they are becoming a regular distraction and sometimes even a point of contention between him and the other students.

Eno's "iceberg" might look something like this:

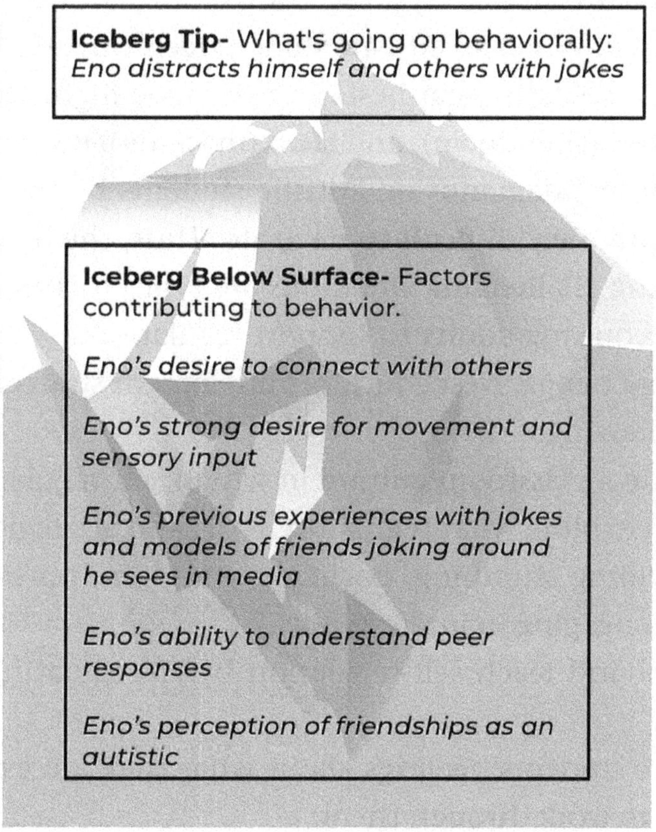

Iceberg Tip- What's going on behaviorally:
Eno distracts himself and others with jokes

Iceberg Below Surface- Factors contributing to behavior.

Eno's desire to connect with others

Eno's strong desire for movement and sensory input

Eno's previous experiences with jokes and models of friends joking around he sees in media

Eno's ability to understand peer responses

Eno's perception of friendships as an autistic

FIGURE 10.5. Enzo's iceberg

Once the function of a behavior is identified, we must continue exploring to try to determine the origin of the function. Delahooke distinguishes between behaviors that occur intentionally and with thought and those that are more reflexive and subconscious. She calls willful behavior that is learned and honed over time "top-down" while behaviors that occur from within more as responses to stress are called "bottom-up." Understanding the origin of specific behaviors will help in understanding how to problem-solve through a challenging situation. The polyvagal theory (Porges 1994) guides us to determine distinctions in the origins of behavior that are particularly helpful when working with autistic students. Dr Porges's theory describes three states that are commonly seen in humans: social engagement, defense (flight or fight), and life threat (shut down). The first is one where a human is in a "good" place, feeling safe and able to function without any threats to their safety. The other two describe what happens to the body automatically when it feels unsafe or feels some kind of threat. The perceived threat may be external or coming from an internal signal in their brain such as anxiety. These states have not been widely studied in autistics, but we do often see autistic response mechanisms taking these last two forms when their autonomic nervous systems are stressed. When an autistic student feels threatened or psychologically unsafe, some common response manifestations include flight (elopement or hiding), fight (aggression), freeze (shut down), and fawn (masking). Because of the nature of an allistic normed world, the demands on autistic students by their social and environmental context are extremely difficult to navigate. Thus, the behaviors that occur for autistic students during challenging situations are typically not choiceful but from a "bottom-up" origin, requiring adults to support regulation as opposed to supporting behavior reshaping or change. Nest educators implement strategies that support regulation, such as the following:

- Teachers cultivate a classroom culture in which self-regulating is discussed and space is given to explore what regulatory tools and strategies work best for each individual, including stimming, pacing, zoning out, putting their head down, deep breathing, engaging in interests, etc.
- Educators model and teach self-regulation by co-regulating, side by side, with their students.
- Teachers validate students' feelings about what they are experiencing, and support is provided to work through them.

- Teachers model regulatory language/behaviors, e.g., using self-talk, "I am feeling frustrated right now because___, so I am going to ___."
- Support is provided to help develop students' self-awareness around learning.
    - How do they prefer to learn, with a partner or alone?
    - Do they prefer to type or write by hand?
    - Does the length of the product matter?
- Teachers plan breaks and downtime throughout the day.
- Access to break areas is provided non-contingently to support regulation.

Partnering with Students

Collaborative approaches produce more lasting solutions than a focus on compliance. Nest practitioners collaborate with students to understand their perspective, the underlying causes of their behavior, and why certain situations throughout the day can be challenging for autistic students. This is an opportunity to take on the role of Guest. (See chapter 9.) Being a guest in these situations involves active listening, asking why, and holding back one's own perspective to give space for students to present their own. During these conversations, there is a focus on highlighting various perspectives and contexts. All people struggle to see others' perspectives when in distress and/or when they do not share neurotype or similar experiences (See "Double Empathy Theory," chapter 4), so sharing perspectives can help reduce distress and open the door to problem-solving and connection.

Nest teams also partner with students to determine solutions to address challenging situations. The Nest Model leans heavily on the work of Dr. Ross Greene (2016) while providing ways to actively include students when working through challenges. Dr. Greene's CPS model, Collaborative and Proactive Solutions, provides a step-by-step guide on how to actually balance the power in the conversation and get authentic collaboration from students. Generally, collaborative navigation of challenges begins with the student getting space to explain their perspective on the challenge. The adult uses questioning techniques to make the student feel respected and valued in this conversation and holds back on providing any kind of feedback or judgment until it is their turn to explain their perspective. Neither perspective is viewed as correct, but the needs of both are discussed in a balanced manner. Finally, the two parties come up with ideas or "solutions" they both feel comfortable with moving forward. It is not top-down where the adult gives the student a list of things to do next time; rather, it is a true collaboration of ideas that will potentially help navigate the same or a similar challenging situation more easily. Time is spent on planning for implementation and support based on the student's developmental needs. Both parties check in and follow up on the plan when necessary.

Nest educators support self-advocacy and interdependence across grade levels. Through co-regulation, modeling, conversations, and joint exploration, Nest educators support students in developing self-awareness about their needs and tools that work for them. They support students to feel confident advocating for what they need and recognizing that we live in an interdependent world in which we all rely on tools, technology, people, and resources to support us every day. At the same time, they are cognizant of the diverse ways students express their advocacy. For example, a student under stress may scream or cry in order to get the attention and help they need; we cannot expect them to just receive that attention or ask for it in the "appropriate" manner. A student under stress does not have access to all of their skills and might be deferring to a scream or cry because that is all they have at the moment and they need us to help co-regulate. By pressuring autistic students to always advocate in a specific or "appropriate" manner, we put extra pressure and expectation on them to have deeper self-awareness than might be developmentally available. Therefore, practitioners work to anticipate and meet needs, coregulate and support, and not demand more out of those who are already experiencing continuing stress.

Role of Data Collection

Nest teams collaborate to determine the function of a behavior in order to establish proactive and supportive response plans. Often, the team will collect specific data to help inform their understanding of the function and origin of a behavior. On occasion, Nest teams use functional behavior assessment, resulting in a Behavior Intervention Plan to support students. However, more commonly, Nest teachers use informal data collection and leverage the expertise across their Nest team, from each practitioner's unique lens, as well as insight from the family and the student to inform their approach. Both direct measures of data collection (data that is gathered from observation) and indirect measures of data collection (data that is gathered by way of interview or questioning) are important to understanding. Nest educators make general observations and take notes on key contextual factors about the situation, e.g., what was going on before and after, possible environmental triggers, who was involved, and what was said/done. From these notes, the educator may begin to see patterns and identify important dimensions of behavior that might be worth investigating further. After the preliminary data is collected, that information is brought to the interdisciplinary Nest team and discussed via a student case conference, using a multi-perspective and strengths-based problem-solving approach.

Let's explore how data might be useful in the case of the student Eno. Teachers and other adults who work with Eno might make a simple anecdotal chart to help understand Eno's "joke-telling" behavior a bit better. This might involve his teachers jotting down the time and circumstance under which "joke telling" occurs (i.e., during what periods or subjects, in the middle of lessons or as a transition is being made, with what audience) as well as the response it receives (gets some laughs, other children ignore it), and what Eno did immediately afterward. The team would then bring their respective notes together to analyze as a group.

Collaborative Planning and Implementation

The collaborative structure of the Nest Model has been thoroughly discussed in previous chapters, and is of utmost importance to the behavioral approach in Nest, as no one practitioner should navigate a challenging situation on their own. At the case conference, each Nest team member provides insight on what might be going on based on their unique lens, as well as ideas and feedback on tools and strategies that would meet the function and provide necessary support. Despite the individual student focus during data collection and case conferencing, Nest teams primarily create implementation plans that are focused on proactive and whole-class supports. This approach leads to changes that will likely have a much broader and sustaining impact on not only that student but all learners in the classroom. At times, individual strategies may be implemented to meet a specific student's needs. At the team meeting, the team agrees upon a clear, comprehensive, and cohesive implementation plan, delegating roles and responsibilities from roll-out through reflection.

In the case of our example student, Eno, when each practitioner's notes about his "joking" behavior are brought to the team meeting, certain patterns might become evident. For example, team members notice that during highly social activities with a clear structure, Eno doesn't rely as much on telling jokes. Maybe team members notice that jokes during transitions and jokes that are directly related to content being taught get more positive responses from peers and are less likely to be a distraction. Thus, strategies relating to these patterns can be formed. Perhaps the team decides to make sure Eno gets many structured opportunities to be social during the day, including having the choice to work in a group for his assignments. They might also find ways to have a "joke corner" during lessons where Eno can be encouraged to tell a joke that relates to the academic topic. The SDI provider might decide to have some sessions where students practice telling jokes and what to do when certain jokes don't go over well.

Monitor and Assess Implementation

Oftentimes, practitioners collect massive amounts of data when things are going wrong or when they encounter challenges, but not in order to follow up on strategies to implement in their classrooms. Hard data can well be useful in learning whether something is supportive or helpful in the school setting.

Once a plan or strategy is settled upon, with both the collaborative team and the student, the team establishes a quick way of checking whether the new strategy is in place as planned and the intervention is working as expected. This is an iterative process. Sometimes the data shows the plan is not working as anticipated and the interdisciplinary team reflects and recalibrates at another team meeting. At other times, the plan is working but the data shows that additional support is needed. Then, teams keep records of strategies that are supportive, which helps keep practitioners on track and motivated. These records can also be used in partnership with students to increase self-awareness. Teaching students to recognize certain things about themselves may pave the way toward self-advocacy.

To come back to our student example, teachers and other practitioners find that Eno loves having a special moment at the end of a mini-lesson to tell a joke related to that day's content. His peers also love it when he takes the spotlight at the end of a lesson, and they are eager to hear his jokes. Then, Eno's teachers speak with him privately to highlight how much the class enjoys his jokes when they are related to what they have been learning. Through these discussions, Eno's likely to become more aware of the social context, which might inform his choices moving forward. For example, Eno may ask his teachers about what they will be learning the next day and try to think of jokes related to those topics, while starting to reduce jokes during other times of the day that were not as successful.

Motivation Systems

While motivation systems—things like marble jars and star charts—can be fun and motivating for students, it is important to remember that there should be additional measures. They may need to be differentiated for your neurodivergent students, and they will not address all behavior. It is also strongly recommended that they be used on a whole-group level as opposed to only with individuals. There are many benefits of sending the message that we are a community and we work together. Individual systems tend to backfire and become punishing for those who are unable to earn or buy in.

PBIS Systems in Nest Schools

Sometimes schools already have well-thought-out and effective PBIS (positive behavior interventions and supports) systems that they would like to keep in place and/or combine with the Nest methodologies. Here are some considerations if you are trying to align your school's current PBIS system with Nest's philosophical foundations. Start with the expectations:

- Are they concrete and specific?
- Are they accepting of diverse cultures and neurotypes?
- What's your reason for requiring them, and can you share them with students in a developmentally relevant way?
- Have they been modeled and explicitly discussed?
- Do kids understand them?

Feel free to make adjustments in your own learning space so that these needs are met. Next, consider execution:

- How are you making sure there are opportunities for every student to earn?
- Did students contribute to the system when issues occur?
- How often are expectations revisited?
- Are they phrased in a positive way?
- Is the visual personalized?
- Is there space for kids to celebrate each other within the system?
- Can there be group, experience-oriented prizes?
- Are there still many opportunities for intrinsic motivation throughout the day (not just for external rewards)?

Don't forget the previous recommendation to have plenty of opportunities for intrinsically motivated activities to be experienced throughout the day, and never withhold an autistic student's interests in order to make the student earn them as a reward.

Conclusion

In the Nest program, behavior support starts with classroom culture. Practitioners strive to create spaces where autistic students belong and are set up for success. Environmental and community supports are put in place proactively to minimize challenges. When challenging situations do occur, practitioners take a thoughtful and collaborative approach to understanding why and then come up with solutions that meet the needs of the whole community.

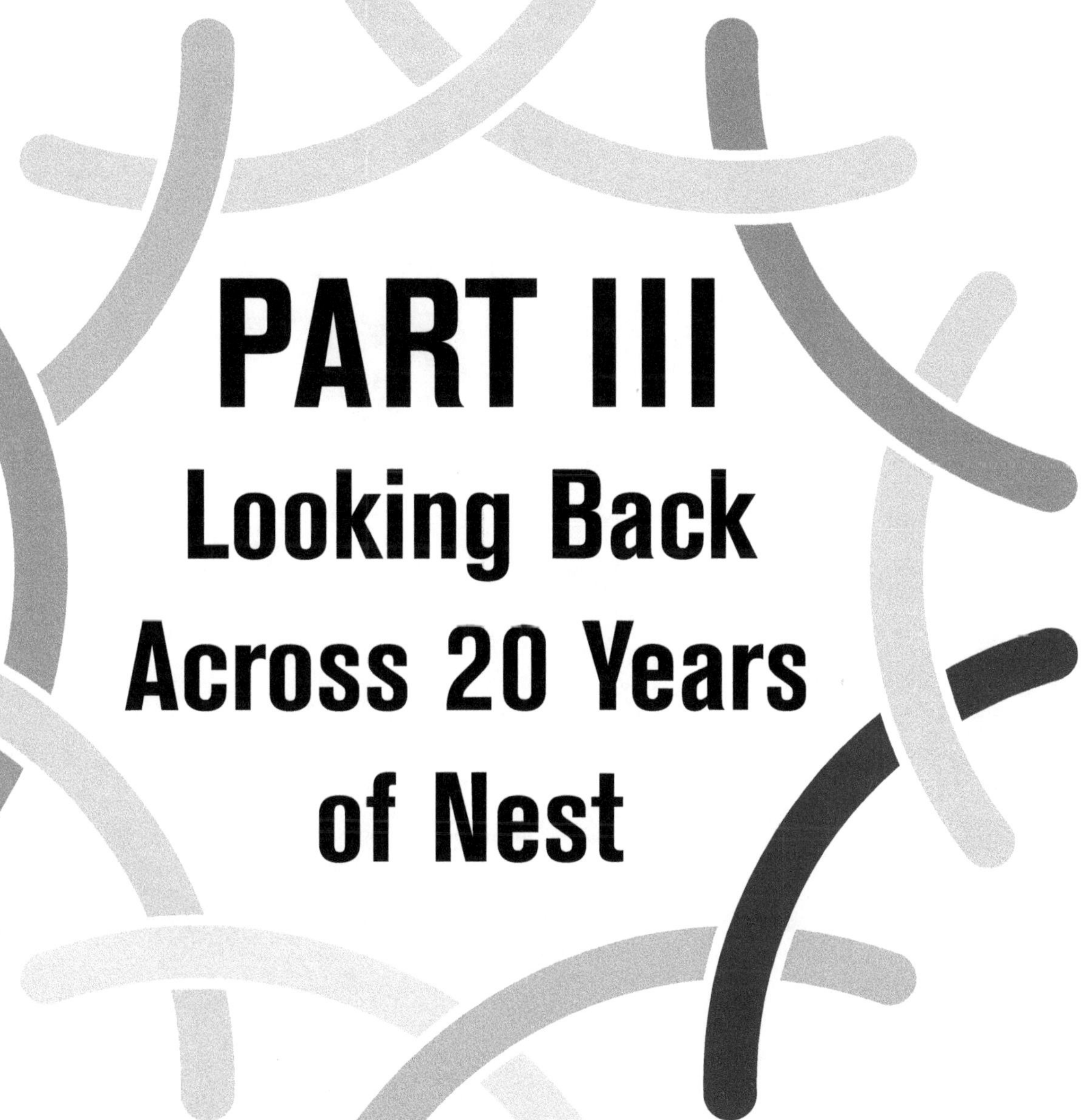

PART III
Looking Back Across 20 Years of Nest

CHAPTER 11

Challenges to Implementation

Dorothy Siegel

The process of launching a new Nest program is complex and necessitates significant thought, time, care and strategy to be successful. Throughout this process, it should be expected that numerous challenges will arise, as they did when the Nest Model was being developed in the New York City Public Schools as well as in other school systems that asked for our assistance with implementation. Some of the implementation challenges faced in New

York City were unique to that city and may not be relevant in other systems, but many of the challenges are broadly applicable and can be used by other districts as learning experiences.

Launching Nest in any public school system is a major effort that requires thoughtful planning to anticipate what the implementation challenges will be and how to work to address them. Below, we discuss some of the major challenges that school leaders anywhere will likely encounter, as well as suggestions about how to overcome them.

1. **Staff and families may embrace outdated and counterproductive notions of inclusion where special education is seen as a "place."**

   Many people think of "inclusion" as what results when students with disabilities are placed in general education classrooms where, it is hoped, they will be able to handle the expectations—social, emotional, academic, and sensory as well as peer interactions—encountered in the classroom. The onus of figuring out how to function in the general education classroom is placed squarely on the student, whose disability in and of itself often makes successful inclusion extremely difficult. This type of "inclusion" views the student through the lens of the medical model of disability, not the social model of disability. (See chapter 4.) Included students are more likely to be successful if the "place" where they are included practices authentic inclusion—where the school's professionals and other staff have made a paradigm shift to view the child through a social disability lens. All else flows from making this shift. Autistic students feel seen, heard, valued, and truly welcome. Nest staff, other school staff, school leaders, school families, ancillary school personnel, and district administrators must buy into this belief system and be trained on the inclusive mindset and social model of disability; they must share in the collaborative inclusion effort at the core of the Nest Model. Without this shift in understanding, behavior, and practices, authentic inclusion is not possible, and students may not be successfully included in mainstream settings.

2. **School and district structures may not support the Nest Model.**

   Many structures and practices that are baked into school systems institutionalize what is and is not possible to implement in that system. These structures and practices are dictated by federal/state/district mandates, union contracts, or political considerations, community values and expectations, existing job descriptions and practices, and the financial and personnel resources available for schools. Proposed school innovations like Nest may be perceived as threatening and/or impermanent, lasting only as long as the superintendent's job contract. Perhaps the biggest obstacle to the successful implementation of a school reform such as Nest is the "we don't do things that way" attitude, which can harden into resistance to innovation. These obstacles can present an almost impenetrable wall of opposition to a school reform like Nest.

   The Nest developers found ways to work with or overcome the institutional obstacles we confronted. We demonstrated to practitioners and system leadership that Nest is better for students, staff, and schools, and more cost-effective. For example, we made common cause with the teacher and principal unions who helped us understand what could and could not be done under their contracts with the city. Once the unions understood what Nest was about and realized that Nest did not challenge their contractual practices, they became champions of the Nest Model. Why? It turns out that teachers, therapists, and administrators, as well as union leaders, truly appreciate Nest's underlying philosophical beliefs and the respect and professional autonomy Nest offers education professionals. They value collaboration with their peers to devise effective strategies and then share in student success. Most practitioners who come into the Nest world love the work, feel supported and appreciated, and want to continue to work in Nest. That positive feedback loop among practitioners at every level cements Nest's place in the system and helps tear down the walls of opposition.

It was important that Nest developers demonstrate to New York City policymakers that Nest is cost-effective. One common practice in education is to allocate individual IEP paraprofessionals as an inclusion support to help students succeed academically and socially. However, in our experience, the assignment of paraprofessionals to individual students is expensive and counterproductive to authentic inclusion. Often, people in the system do not realize the extensive cost associated with this practice nor the deleterious effect of relying on a paraprofessional instead of teachers to support the most complex cases.

Another common practice is the mandating of an excessive number of services on students' IEPs in the mistaken belief that "more is better." More services are not better, but they do raise the cost of serving those children. Working in the Nest therapeutic classroom, trained teachers can often provide better support, more cohesively and cost-effectively.

The Nest Model's interdisciplinary approach—with smaller class size and highly trained co-teachers and therapists—is not only superior, but its cost compares favorably with the cost of autistic students placed in any other setting. In New York City in the days before Nest was an option, most autistic students were placed in District 75, a separate district for students with low-incidence disabilities, where the cost per student is roughly three times greater than for a student in a neighborhood school. Wanting to avoid placement in a District 75 or other NYCPS setting, many New York City parents unilaterally placed their students in non-public schools and then sued NYCPS for tuition reimbursement, transportation, and legal fees. As a result, New York City spent millions of dollars more on payment to private schools than it would have allocated to public school programs. Public school leaders recognized that Nest is more successful and more cost-effective than the alternatives for most children with autism. They institutionalized funding mechanisms that are tied to the Nest structures outlined in this book. Today, the Nest program is a standard placement option for autistic students in New York City public schools.

School systems typically contract on an ad-hoc basis with external organizations to meet the professional development needs of their staff. In New York, NYCPS established a partnership with NYU in recognition of its demonstrated value in providing program development, staff training, continuing professional development, and on-site support, all necessary to the ongoing success of the Nest program. This arrangement is cost-effective; the cost of all these professional development activities from NYU for all Nest staff was only about $2,000 per year per Nest student.

One of the most satisfying ways to break down systemic barriers is to have a core group of allies advocating for your program. In New York, dedicated Nest parents went to great lengths to ensure the Nest program had such allies. Parents advocated for Nest to local elected officials when inevitable competing priorities threatened the funding or fidelity of the program. These elected officials, wishing to demonstrate support for the families in their district, became champions of what they saw as a successful educational program. In this kind of positive environment, institutional resistance to Nest melted away and morphed into the kind of broad support that Nest enjoys today in New York City.

3. **Even well-meaning and well-trained teachers, therapists, and administrators don't necessarily know how to "do authentic inclusion" with autistic students, especially in collaboration with their colleagues in other disciplines.**

   In their professional training, many teachers, therapists, and administrators don't study either the basics of teaching autistic students or their inclusion, and what they learn about these subjects is likely to be superficial. Furthermore, their professional education is unlikely to include training on how to work across disciplines. Even colleagues in the same school typically have different mindsets about autism and inclusion thanks to their dissimilar professional training and experiences; the approaches and strategies they use may be unfamiliar to their peers. This is an inefficient and ineffectual state of affairs and is confusing for the students.

   Nest training and professional supports ensure that all Nest schools practice authentic inclusion while implementing the Nest Model with fidelity. Furthermore, the Nest collaborative team approach ensures that all professionals are on the same page on elements of practice. Nest trainings are coordinated to promote consistent approaches within and across the disciplines. Internally consistent practices are an essential feature of Nest.

4. **Per-class funding in inclusion settings can seem to be costly, unpredictable, and often not cost-effective.**

   Per-class funding of inclusive classes is typically a function of (1) the number and ratio of students with and without IEPs, (2) the provision of mandated related services and paraprofessionals for individual students, and (3) the number of mandated sessions they require. Generally, the number and ratio of students with and without IEPs may fluctuate; the total number of students in the class may vary; and the number of mandates may change from year to year. In short, funding can be ad hoc and variable, based as it is on the totality of identified needs and mandated services, in addition to the basic cost of teachers and paraprofessionals. Further, in New York City, inclusion classes tend to be relatively large—about the same size as general education classes or larger.

   In contrast, Nest had a specified per-class allocation based on an inviolable class size and ratio, a relatively small class size that ensures both consistent and adequate funding, and class size/ratio stability from year to year. Nest elementary classes have two teachers, a set number of autistic students (four or five), and a set number of students without IEPs (eight in the lower grades to sixteen in the upper grades). Paraprofessionals are not included in the classroom model, and, with very limited exceptions, there are no one-to-one paraprofessionals assigned for students. The stability and consistency of funding, the small class size, and the low ratio of IEP to non-IEP students—all integral features of the Nest Model—help create the conditions for a maximally effective therapeutic classroom environment.

   Probably the largest cost savings built into the Nest Model is the lack of both programmatic and IEP-mandated paraprofessionals in the classroom. Non-Nest classrooms in New York often have an IEP-mandated paraprofessional assigned to one or more autistic students, adding greatly to the per-class cost. *(The cost for salary and benefits of a paraprofessional in NYCPS is close to half the cost of a teacher.)* In the Nest program, given the relatively small class size and the ongoing professional training and support, Nest teachers, in collaboration with Nest's related service providers, offer whatever support Nest students need. There is no need for paraprofessional support.

Speech pull-outs are rarely necessary in Nest because the speech therapy that autistic students need is provided in SDI small group sessions, which are a programmatic support serving all Nest autistic students. Non-Nest inclusion classes have students with a variety of disabilities and needs and are mandated for various different group and individual sessions, spread across the day. SDI is a much more appropriate and less disruptive way of meeting the speech needs of autistic students. Since OTs and social workers participate in Nest team meetings, they can offer professional advice and provide indirect services through discussions with classroom teachers, eliminating the need for some individual or small group OT and/or counseling mandates.

5. **There may be a strong temptation to water down the implementation of the Nest Model in response to system challenges.**

   Stuff happens! Especially in public school systems! Challenges do arise when municipalities cut their schools' budgets, when other school needs compete with the Nest program's requirements, or when individual students or staff members present unexpectedly difficult challenges to the implementation of Nest with fidelity. School leadership may have to decide what to cut back, change, or substitute. In the twenty-plus-year history of Nest, we have encountered numerous system-wide and school-specific challenges. The Nest Model is comprehensive, cohesive, and cost-effective, but in order to produce excellent results, it needs to be implemented with fidelity. Indeed, Nest is like a rubber band ball, composed of many different types of rubber bands (the elements of Nest) all working together and relying on each other to produce the "bounce" that is the magic of a well-oiled Nest program. Pulling out an element here and changing an element there significantly affects the outcome and damages the cohesiveness of the model as a whole, ultimately altering the ability of the program to create Nest "magic." Small and temporary tweaks can be made to accommodate unexpected situations, but it is essential to refer back to the model to find solutions that sustain its fidelity and thus best sustain Nest's "bounce."

6. **Access to the Nest program may not be equitable.**

When the Nest founders first conceived of creating a program to serve autistic students in an inclusive setting, others suggested establishing it as a private or charter school. "It will be a lot easier to pull that off," they said. "You'll never get the Board of Ed to so radically change the way they do things." But the founders did not want to found a boutique private program for students from more advantaged families who had access to the new program. They wanted any model they developed to change how the education of autistic students is done in New York City, to become an integral part of the local public school system, and to ensure *equitable* access for *all* New York City families. From the very beginning, the purpose of the model was to change the trajectory of all autistic students' lives, no matter their zip code.

The vast size of NYCPS made it difficult for families to become aware of the program in its early days. Once aware of the Nest option, families with autistic students needed a Nest program near their home. However, even if families were aware that a Nest program school existed near them, their local Committee on Special Education—which made the placement offers—may not have been aware of the Nest program's existence. In 2004, when deputy chancellor Carmen Farina announced that there would be a Nest program in every one of the thirty-two NYC sub-districts, the program began to expand everywhere. She charged the NYCPS with creating new Nest sites to ensure equitable access for all NYC students.

NYCPS has continued to reassess and improve the accessibility of its internal systems. All relevant school personnel—i.e., psychologists, social workers, principals, supervisors, and sub-district superintendents—were trained and are now expected to be conversant with Nest and other centrally supported autism programs in neighborhood schools. The autism program application process is now simpler and more accessible, requiring only that families express their interest by submitting basic information via a digital form available on the NYCPS public website. In addition, NYCPS conducts regular outreach to early childhood programs and agencies that serve families with autistic students. In recent years, NYCPS has intentionally sought out underserved neighborhoods in which to locate Nest and other specialized autism programs. All of this demonstrates NYCPS's firm commitment that all New York City autistic students will have equitable access to an inclusive evidence-based autism program in a neighborhood school. We suggest that other public school districts implementing Nest seriously consider measures that ensure Nest's accessibility to all autistic students in their district.

7. **It is neither simple nor intuitive to understand how to launch a new program that upends many fundamental assumptions of special education practice.**

   In the earliest days, Nest developers established an ASD Planning and Implementation Committee that studied the research findings of Cynthia Coburn (2003) on successful scaling up of school reform models. (See sidebar.) Using her findings as a guide, the developers adjusted the elements of the initial pilot program to the realities of school practices in New York City, and vice versa. The pilot, a nascent model, changed repeatedly. One year later, when Nest began to expand to new schools, the developers once again used Coburn's research as an invaluable guide to help the model line up with school system realities.

   When a school reform program has been launched and is deemed to be successful, there is a temptation to rush scaling it up to serve more students in more schools. It can be tempting to open new programs before all necessary Nest elements are in place and solidified.

Successful School Reform

Dorothy Siegel

In 2003, when we were developing the Nest Model, I came across the work of Cynthia E. Coburn, an education researcher who had synthesized the literature on school reform models. In a 2003 article in Educational Researcher,[1] she described how the research on school reform often consisted of simply counting how many new programs had been created using a particular model, without sufficient attention being paid to the nature and quality of the reform or whether its effect was deep and lasting. In her view, reformers must "move beyond the numbers" in order to make deep and lasting change in schooling. Coburn identified the four essential dimensions necessary for successful school reform: spread of norms, principles, and beliefs; depth of change; reform ownership; and sustainability. I was inspired by her analysis and made it the operational theory that guided the development of all aspects of the emerging Nest Model and its citywide replication. The following are the lessons I learned from Coburn's four essential dimensions and which I see as vital to the expansion, sustainability, and fidelity of Nest.

1. **Spread of norms, principles, and beliefs:** Change must involve more than the spread of activity structures, materials, and classroom organization. Teachers and schools are more likely to

But if the launch of a Nest program is rushed, compromises will inevitably be made, and the program will not be implemented with depth and fidelity. Significant care must be taken and strategic planning must be done to ensure that the comprehensive Nest Model is scaled in its totality. The work of transforming a neighborhood school into a Nest school takes time. In our experience, it takes two to three years for Nest-inclusive practices and habits of mind to become sufficiently embedded in a school that it begins to feel like a permanent change. Professionals across the school begin to change their mindsets to one of authentic inclusion. Nest practices begin to permeate the school. It takes another two or three years for the program to completely "age up" to the school's last grade. With continual support and training along the way, outdated habits and thinking may be kept at bay. We urge school districts interested in launching Nest to expect that deep, permanent change will take time. Rushing the process may result in incomplete and flawed implementation and diminished results.

be able to sustain and deepen reform over time when school and district policy and priorities are compatible or aligned with reform. Spreading reform norms, beliefs, and principles within schools and districts may be a key mechanism for *developing this normative coherence.*

2. **Depth of change:** Reforms must effect deep and consequential change in classroom practice as a result of *changes in teachers' beliefs, norms of social interaction, and underlying pedagogical principles* as enacted in the curriculum.

3. **Reform ownership:** Teachers, school leadership, and district leadership *need to exercise reform-centered decision-making* as they work to sustain practice in the face of new circumstances, initiatives, and priorities that may or may not conflict with the reform.

4. **Sustainability:** Teachers are better able to sustain change when there are *mechanisms in place at multiple levels of the system to support their efforts.* This includes the presence of a supportive professional community of colleagues in the school that reinforces normative changes and provides continuing opportunities to learn, knowledgeable and supportive school leadership, connections with other schools or teachers engaged in similar reform, and normative coherence or alignment between the district policy context and the reform.

1. Cynthia E. Coburn, "Rethinking Scale: Moving Beyond Numbers to Deep and Lasting Change." *Educational Researcher*, Vol.32, No.6, pp.3-12 (August/September 2003).

CHAPTER 12

Outcomes and Future Perspectives

Dorothy Siegel and Allison Graham Brown

Nest works. Twenty years ago, our pilot sought to answer the question, "Is it possible to create a model for the inclusive education of autistic students in neighborhood schools that can meaningfully work in the New York City Public School system?" The years since the pilot began have continually reinforced the answer: "Yes, there is, and that model is Nest." In the 2023–2024 school year, the number of Nest schools grew to eighty-three, with the capacity to serve 1,979 autistic students alongside 4,432 non-autistic learners in hundreds of inclusive public school classrooms. The Nest Model has demonstrated that it is an impactful, sustainable, and scalable inclusion model for the public education of autistic students. Across the years, through surveys and assessments, outcome data, anecdotes, and shared stories, it became clear that Nest works for the students we serve, it works for the Nest families, it works for the Nest program staff, and it works for the school communities in which Nest is embedded. And so, after twenty years, we believe that not only is the Nest Model right for NYC but that it can be used to improve the special education landscape across the country.

The Autism Nest classroom is specifically designed to meet both the academic and therapeutic needs of autistic learners. The Nest Model makes use of the same academic curricula as other classes on a given grade level; schools hosting the Nest program hold the same academic expectations for Nest students as for their typically developing peers. The model provides the structure, support, and programming to achieve successful inclusion without compromising academic rigor, while also meeting the sensory, social, and behavioral needs of its students (Koenig et al. 2009). The Nest Model is designed to foster success in all these areas.

The previous chapters outlined how Nest came to be, discussed what elements are essential to implementing the model with fidelity, and described considerations for implementation in new locations. In this chapter, we discuss recent outcome data that speak to the efficacy of the Nest Model and reinforce how Nest works!

Student Achievement

New York City Public Schools (NYCPS) has tracked student data to make comparative assessments between autistic students in Nest programs and their autistic peers who are served in typical NYCPS Integrated Co-Teaching or special classes. Here are some highlights from their findings:

- According to NYC public school officials, 95 percent of children who attend Nest programs graduate from high school, more than 30 percentage points higher than other NYCPS students with disabilities (Zimmerman, 2024).
- In 2021–2022, Nest students were more than three times as likely to score proficient on Grade 3–8 NYS English Language Arts (ELA) and Math exams compared to the autistic students in other Integrated Co-Teaching or special classes.
- Nest students have consistently higher attendance rates compared to autistic students receiving instruction in other Integrated Co-Teaching or special classes.

School Staff Feedback

In order to assess, learn, and reflect on the Nest Model to improve the program and its impact, the NYU Nest Support Project requests feedback from Nest staff. This annual process enables us to refine our model as new research emerges, as the field evolves, and in response to the experiences of those key stakeholders, helping to ensure that we remain an exemplar for the inclusive education of autistic students.

One of the major supports built into the Nest Model is the consultant. At the end of each school year, the NYU Nest Support Project sends a (anonymous) survey to all Nest school staff to solicit feedback related to the consultation support provided across the year. In the 2023–2024 school year, 628 Nest staff responded to this survey. Of those who had direct contact with a Nest Support Project consultant, to the question, "How would you rate the support from your Nest consultant this year?" over 85 percent said the service they received was "extremely helpful or very helpful." The survey also asked about ways in which Nest consultation was provided:

In which way(s) did your Nest consultant support your school? (Select all that apply) 46

Q6.4 - In which way(s) did your Nest consultant support your school? (Select all that apply) - Selected Choice	Percentage
Attending team meetings	70%
Presenting a PD	37%
1:1 or small group consultation	72%
Providing asynchronous or Google Form responses	17%
Remote classroom visits	4%
In-Person Classroom Visits	96%

FIGURE 12.1. Data from Nest staff survey

A small sample of common responses is shown below:

> *"Support has been amazing; our consultants are always available to troubleshoot and problem-solve in a practical manner. They quickly replied to all inquiries and shared information and visuals to support me."*
>
> *—Anonymous*

> *"My consultant was able to help with my first year as a Nest therapist by helping me through things that were difficult, giving me feedback, and giving me different ways to support my Nest students. She made me feel more confident in the therapy that I was providing."*
>
> *—Nest SLP*

> *"Our consultant is always extremely resourceful and insightful."*
>
> *—Nest social worker*

"I loved how our consultants helped us think about our present strengths and also how to continue improving in the future, as a program. She helped us analyze what is working at the moment and how we can continue cultivating it for the upcoming school year."

—*Nest administrator*

"Creating a coaching schedule, visiting classes and sharing best practices, teacher feedback—and literally everything provided is amazing and has been such a great support!!"

—*Nest Coach*

Every new staff member is required to take a basic course on autism and the Nest program, given under the aegis of the Nest program. In the spring 2024 semester, 119 Nest staff members took the NYU 701 Autism course, and each was asked to complete a course evaluation; 55 responded. The first series of questions used a Likert scale of 1–5 to assess the gains they perceived from participation in the course: no gains, slight gains, moderate gains, significant gains, great gains. None of the respondents indicated that they had not made any gains or had only made slight gains in understanding of Nest's philosophical beliefs and how they impact daily practice. Additionally, 100 percent of respondents indicated that they gained the ability to set up a classroom environment with Nest student's sensory needs in mind, with 61 percent indicating significant gains and 30 percent indicating great gains.

Even more compelling were the responses to the open-ended question in which the course participants were asked to share their biggest takeaway. Most highlighted the paradigm shift toward the Nest lens on how they think about autism and inclusion. Here is a sample of responses reflective of common themes:

"My biggest takeaway is learning that things are not always as they look, and it is so important to dig deeper, observe more closely, listen thoroughly in order to understand the source and function of a student's behavior. As a teacher, to slow down in reaction."

"I think my biggest takeaway is that autistic people do not have to change or that we have to help them adapt to this 'normal' society, but rather we have to make

> *room in our minds and society to meet with them and understand the way they see the world."*
>
> *"This class has made me more passionate about working with students with autism, and I have gained a greater appreciation of all they bring to class."*
>
> *"BE OPEN , OBSERVANT, AND MINDFUL!"*
>
> *"This course was excellent! My biggest takeaway is to always try to learn and be up-to-date, as strategies/tools tried in the past are not always neurodiversity-affirming."*
>
> *"My biggest takeaway is that we always need to be on the lookout for how we can make modifications in our classroom environment, teaching, and social awareness to meet the needs of our autistic students. It is not their job to adjust to our environment, and often when we make these kinds of changes, all students benefit."*

In 2022, the Research Alliance for New York City Schools conducted a qualitative study (N=29) aimed at understanding educators' experiences in the Autism Nest program and how they believe it affected their students, schools, and professional practices (Fanscali and Almash 2022). Here are some key results:

- Respondents unanimously reported that the training courses were useful in preparing them to implement the Nest Model.
  - What respondents cited as most helpful was learning the timing of when to intervene, how to implement behavior intervention systems, and what activities and resources they could use with all children in the classroom.
- When asked about the benefits of the Nest program to the larger school community, teachers and administrators said the overall school culture was more caring, kind, and supportive for both learners and staff.
  - Respondents described how positive school-wide changes took place, both in terms of interpersonal interactions and instructional support and practices.
  - Respondents reported feeling that teachers were more open and flexible and that they used language focused on positives rather than deficits as a result of participating in the Nest program.

Family Satisfaction

Surveys were conducted in June 2023 and June 2024 by NYCPS of fifth- and eighth-grade Nest families (N=328). Families from 97 percent of Nest programs participated in the survey over the course of the two years, and the results showed the following:

- Families reported high levels of satisfaction and a high likelihood of recommending the program to other families of autistic children.
- Ninety-five percent of families reported that their children benefited from the small class sizes in the Autism Nest program.
- Eighty-five percent of families stated that the Nest program helped their child build independence.
- Families valued the strong family-school relationship that the programs offered. An overwhelming majority of fifth grade families agreed that teachers and service providers treated them as partners in educating their child (92 percent) and worked closely with them to meet their child's needs (92 percent)

Nest families have always been an integral part of the Nest program, and therefore their experiences and feedback are vital to shaping the ongoing development of the Nest Model. Over the years, we have had the pleasure of innumerable families reaching out to share their stories and the impact Nest had on their autistic and non-autistic children. Here is a small sample from the past two years. *Please note, names and identifying information have been removed when requested.*

> *My son Dylan was diagnosed with autism at eighteen months and received Early Intervention and CPSE (special education preschool). Dylan was blessed to be accepted into the Nest program. The Nest program is a wonderful program that provided my son with the support, learning, and opportunity to flourish. The social-emotional supports, such as SDI, which helps with improving social functioning, were one of the best experiences Dylan had. SDI gave Dylan a voice and helped him to express himself articulately and from his heart. SDI was a safe space among his peers that unfortunately he doesn't have now. The Nest team is phenomenal, and the teachers are loving, compassionate, and focus on meeting all children where they're at. Dylan went from a non-verbal eighteen-month-old to Valedictorian twice, at his Nest elementary school and then at his Nest*

middle school. The Nest program foundation Dylan received has contributed to him thriving at his current non-Nest school, Brooklyn Technical High School, which has six thousand kids.

—Lucy, parent of a former Nest student (2024)

"The socialization in the SDI club really helped my son to start coming out of his shell and be more independent and take the initiative on things he is interested in."

—Autism Nest parent (2023)

Dear Dorothy and the Nest Support Team,

My son has been in the Nest program since kindergarten, and this June he will graduate from high school. He has come a long way, and so much of his progress is due to the amazing support of the Nest program. His Nest school was his home from K-5, and his new home after that was a Nest middle and high school. His Nest elementary school was/is amazing, and now I would like to add his middle and high school to the amazing chart. The principal and staff are beyond phenomenal. Every encounter with staff and administration was always kind, professional, and real, whether it was involving bumps in the road or celebrating smooth roads. The high school's Nest transition coach goes above and beyond to help all the students learn to navigate their paths. We consider our son's high school staff family and always will!! I cannot believe he is getting ready to start college in September!!! Please let me close by saying a big giant thank-you from the bottom of my heart for the Nest program. This program changed my son's life and my family's too!!! Please keep doing what you do; it works, and its value is immeasurable.

—Parent of a K–12 Nest student (2024)

"We think it's possible to leave Nest because of Nest."

—Autism Nest parent (2023)

Presuming Success

Dr. Kristie Patten

The qualitative and quantitative data presented in this book paint a picture where students are academically successful, families are satisfied, staff feel supported, and the classroom experiences as described are transformative for students. These indicators are key outcomes in the Nest Model. That is only half the story—or maybe 75 percent of the story—as they are critical to the success and sustainability of the model. In addition to outcomes, research done by my colleagues and me shows that the foundational structures and core principles embraced by the Nest program can fundamentally provide support for the idea that autism is a difference, not a deficit. If we create a "high-functioning environment" with an emphasis on what the environment provides versus what is lacking in the individual and rejecting the high vs. low label, all students thrive. The Nest program has created opportunities and high-functioning environments that are related to interests, access, and abilities that don't demand readiness first but rather presume success (Chen and Patten 2021).

FIGURE 12.2. PS 165 Nest Reunion 2024

CHAPTER 12

At PS 165, we pride ourselves on the home-school connection we have with our families. Over the years, we have stayed in touch with many of our graduates and their families. They have shared their continued journeys and successes as they moved on to middle school, high school, and beyond. In June 2023, we were lucky to host a PS 165 Nest Reunion with former students and families. Families came from Queens, Long Island, and even California! One of our first Nest students who attended was finishing up her final year of college and studying developmental disabilities. We heard many success stories of students attending prestigious high schools, such as Bronx Science, Townsend Harris, and Stuyvesant, as well as Hunter College High School. Most importantly, it was so nice to see that friendships have remained and students that lost touch were exchanging numbers. It is our hope to host another reunion to continue keeping in touch with our former students and their families.

—Allison Greene, Nest coach, PS 165 in Queens

Fig Season

An anecdote from Dorothy Siegel

One Sunday afternoon in 2023, I was shopping for groceries at the Park Slope Food Co-op, which always has an amazing array of fresh produce in great variety and abundance. I said to no one in particular, "Oh wow, figs! It must be fig season." A woman standing next to me, also in front of the figs, informed me that the Co-op had *two* varieties of figs, and she recommended one of them. I thanked her. I wasn't at all surprised at this exchange, as Co-op members often swap information about interesting foods and recipes in the produce aisle. In fact, that's how I learned how to prepare uncommon fruits and vegetables like chayote (chop and mix with lime juice, salt, and chili powder) and kiwi berries (cut in half and mix in with fruit salad).

Then she said, "You probably don't remember me. But I know who you are. You're Dorothy Siegel. You started the Nest program. I've met you here at the Co-op a few times over the years and talked with you. My son has been in the Nest program since kindergarten, and now he is a freshman at George Washington University. He's doing great, thanks to the Nest program. I can't thank you enough for creating it. It made all the difference in the world to our family."

Just then, *another* Co-op member standing nearby (near the tomatoes) piped up, "Excuse me. I couldn't help but overhear you. My son is also in the Nest program. It changed my family's life. I am so grateful. Thank you so much."

But then, *yet another* woman (we were in front of the shallots by this time) chimed in, "Pardon me for intruding. I overheard your conversation. My son, too, is in the Nest program, in second grade. I'm so happy to hear from all of you that the Nest program will continue to help him be happy and successful."

We chatted for another minute or two, after which I resumed scrutinizing the figs, tomatoes, and shallots. I half expected to meet another Nest parent, but none appeared. I guess three was enough for one day of shopping at the Co-op. My heart was full.

Conclusion

We remain incredibly proud of the Nest Model and grateful to all who have contributed to both its development and implementation. The Nest community is inspiring, thoughtful, responsive, collaborative, and beautiful in its diversity. The past twenty years have demonstrated the innovative progress, the incredible success, and the dynamic potential of the Nest Model. We can't wait to see what the next twenty years will bring!

REFERENCES

Adkin, T. "Mask on, Mask off. How the Common Understanding of Autistic Masking is Creating Another Mask." *Emergent Divergence*, May 8, 2023. https://emergentdivergence.com/2023/05/08/mask-on-mask-off-how-the-common-understanding-of-autistic-masking-is-creating-another-mask/.

American Psychiatric Association. *Diagnostic and Statistical Manual of Mental Disorders*. 5th ed. Arlington, VA: Author, 2013.

ASD Nest: Exploring Educators' Perspectives on an Innovative Model for Autistic Students. New York, NY: Steinhardt.nyu.edu, November 2022. https://steinhardt.nyu.edu/research-alliance/research/asd-nest-exploring-educators-perspectives-innovative-model-autistic.

Autism West Midlands. "Autism and Stimming." *Autism West Midlands | Supporting the Autistic Community*, 2019. https://www.autismwestmidlands.org.uk/wp-content/uploads/2019/12/Stimming_Nov_2019.pdf.

Autism West Midlands. "Autism and Sensory Issues." *Autism West Midlands | Supporting the Autistic Community*, 2020. https://www.autismwestmidlands.org.uk/wp-content/uploads/2020/02/Sensory_Issues_February_2020.pdf.

Bailin, A. "Clearing Up Some Misconceptions about Neurodiversity." *Scientific American Blogs*, June 6, 2019. https://tinyurl.com/y43ydlm9.

Baranek, G., F. J. David, M. D. Poe, W. L. Stone, and L. R. Watson. "Sensory Experiences Questionnaire: Discriminating Features in Young Children with Autism, Developmental Delays, and Typical Development." *Journal of Child Psychology and Psychiatry & Allied Disciplines* 47, no. 6 (2006): 591-601.

Bennett, J. "Lived Experience and the Limits (and Possibilities) of Empathy." *Cultural Studies Review* 25, no. 2 (2019): 84-88.

Ben-Sasson, A., R. Fluss, S. A. Cermak, B. Engel-Yeger, and E. Gal. "A Meta-Analysis of Sensory Modulation Symptoms in Individuals with Autism Spectrum Disorders." *Journal of Autism and Developmental Disorders* 39, no. 1 (2008): 1-11.

Binns, A. V., and J. O. Cardy. "Developmental Social Pragmatic Interventions for Preschoolers with Autism Spectrum Disorder: A Systematic Review." *Autism & Developmental Language Impairments* 4, no. 1 (2019): 1-18.

Bleiweiss, J., L. Hough, and S. Cohen. *Expanded Classroom Guideposts for the ASD Nest*. Unpublished manuscript, 2011.

Bradshaw, C. P., M. M. Mitchell, and P. J. Leaf. "Examining the Effects of Schoolwide Positive Behavior Interventions and Supports on Student Outcomes." *Journal of Positive Behavior Interventions* 12, no. 3 (2010): 133-148.

Brennan, S., and L. Hough. *Social Development Intervention (SDI) Guideposts*. Unpublished manuscript, 2008.

Brosnan, M., and C. Ashwin. "Thinking, Fast and Slow on the Autism Spectrum." *Autism* 27, no. 5 (2023): 1245-1255. https://doi.org/10.1177/13623613221132437.

Brown, L. "People First - Create an Environment of Respect." *Autistic Hoya*, December 28, 2011. https://www.autistichoya.com/2011/12/people-first-create-environment-of.html.

Buron, K. D., and M. Curtis. *The Incredible 5-Point Scale*. 2nd ed. Shawnee Mission, KS: AAPC Press, 2012.

Calkins, S. D., and S. E. Dedmon. "Physiological and Behavioral Regulation in Two-Year-Old Children with Aggressive/Destructive Behavior Problems." *Journal of Abnormal Child Psychology* 28 (2000): 103-118. https://doi.org/10.1023/A:1005112912906.

Chen, Y. L., and K. Patten. "Shifting Focus from Impairments to Inclusion: Expanding Occupational Therapy for Neurodivergent Students to Address School Environments." *American Journal of Occupational Therapy* 75 (2021): 7503347010. https://doi.org/10.5014/ajot.2020.040618.

Chen, Y. L., L. L. Senande, M. Thorsen, and K. Patten. "Peer Preferences and Characteristics of Same-Group and Cross-Group Social Interactions among Autistic and Non-Autistic Adolescents." *Autism* 25 (2021): 1885–1900. https://doi.org/10.1177/13623613211005918.

Coburn, C. E. "Rethinking Scale: Moving beyond Numbers to Deep and Lasting Change." *Educational Researcher* 32, no. 6 (2003): 3-12.

Cohen, S. "Inclusion of Young Children with Autism Spectrum Disorders: Updates and Other Thoughts." *Autism and Asperger's Digest Magazine*, May-June 2006, 6-11, 18-19, 31.

Cohen, S. *Targeting Autism: What We Know, Don't Know, and Can Do to Help Young Children with Autism Spectrum Disorders*. 3rd ed. Berkeley, CA: University of California Press, 2006.

Cohen, S., and J. Bleiweiss. *Guideposts for Staff of the ASD Nest Program*. Unpublished manuscript, 2007.

Cohen, S., and L. Hough, eds. *The ASD Nest Model*. Shawnee Mission, KS: AAPC, 2013.

Deci, E. L., and R. M. Ryan. *Intrinsic Motivation and Self-Determination in Human Behavior*. New York, NY: Plenum, 1985.

Dee, T. S., and M. R. West. "The Non-Cognitive Returns to Class Size." *Educational Evaluation and Policy Analysis* 33, no. 1 (2011): 23-46. https://doi.org/10.3102/0162373710392370.

Delahooke, M. *Beyond Behaviors: Using Brain Science and Compassion to Understand and Solve Children's Behavioral Challenges*. Hachette UK, 2019.

Dunlap, G., R. Iovannone, K. J. Wilson, D. K. Kincaid, and P. Strain. "Prevent-Teach-Reinforce: A Standardized Model of School-Based Behavioral Intervention." *Journal of Positive Behavioral Interventions* 12 (2010): 9-22.

Dunn, W., B. S. Myles, and S. Orr. "Sensory Processing Issues Associated with Asperger Syndrome: A Preliminary Investigation." *American Journal of Occupational Therapy* 56, no. 1 (2002): 97-102.

Doyle, N. "We Have Been Disabled: How The Pandemic Has Proven The Social Model Of Disability." *Forbes*, April 29, 2020. https://www.forbes.com/sites/drnancydoyle/2020/04/29/we-have-been-disabled-how-the-pandemic-has-proven-the-social-model-of-disability/.

Edwards, C. P., L. Gandini, and G. E. Forman. "Connecting through Caring and Learning Spaces." In *The Hundred Languages of Children: The Reggio Emilia Approach to Early Childhood Education*, 3rd ed., Westpoint, Conn: Praeger, 1993.

Ellzey, L. M. "Autistic Care: Communication Differences." *Autinelle Instagram*. Retrieved June 3, 2024. https://www.instagram.com/p/CpYE1cduAtX/?img_index=10.

Fanscali, C., and F. Almash. *ASD Nest: Exploring Educators' Perspectives on an Innovative Model for Autistic Students*. New York, NY: NYU Steinhardt, 2022. https://steinhardt.nyu.edu/research-alliance/research/asd-nest-exploring-educators-perspectives-innovative-model-autistic.

REFERENCES

Fine, L. "Cracking the Shell." *Education Week* 21, no. 12 (2001): 22-27.

Friend, M., and L. Cook. *Interactions: Collaboration Skills for School Professionals.* 7th ed. Boston, MA: Prentice Hall, 2012.

Gardiner, F. "First-Hand Perspectives on Behavioral Interventions for Autistic People and People with other Developmental Disabilities." Office of Developmental Primary Care Improving Outcomes for People with Developmental Disabilities. Washington, DC: Autistic Self Advocacy Network (ASAN), 2017. https://autisticadvocacy.org/wp-content/uploads/2017/05/Behavioral-Interventions-Report-Final.pdf.

Gates Foundation. *American Teachers on the Teaching Professions.* Retrieved from https://www.scholastic.com/primarysources/pdfs/Gates2012_full.pdf, 2012.

Gerber, S. "A Developmental Perspective on Language Assessment and Intervention for Children on the Autistic Spectrum." *Topics in Language Disorders* 23, no. 2 (2003): 74-94.

Grandin, T. *Thinking in Pictures: My Life with Autism.* New York, NY: Vintage Books, 1995.

Gray, C. *The New Social Story™ Book: Revised and Expanded 10th Anniversary Edition.* Arlington, TX: Future Horizons, 2010.

Green, S. A., and A. Ben-Sasson. "Anxiety Disorders and Sensory Over-Responsivity in Children with Autism Spectrum Disorders: Is There a Causal Relationship?" *Journal of Autism and Developmental Disorders* 40, no. 12 (2010): 1495-1504.

Greene, R. W. *Lost and Found: Helping Behaviorally Challenging Students (and, While You're at It, All the Others).* Hoboken, NJ: Jossey-Bass, 2016.

Greenspan, S. I., and S. Wieder. *Engaging Autism: Using the Floortime Approach to Help Children Relate, Communicate, and Think.* Boston, MA: Da Capo Press, 2006.

Gutstein, S. *Autism Aspergers, Solving the Relationship Puzzle: A New Developmental Program That Opens the Door to Lifelong Social & Emotional Growth.* Future Horizons, 2000.

Haigh, S. M., J. A. Walsh, C. A. Mazefsky, N.J. Minshew, and S. M. Eack. "Processing Speed is Impaired in Adults with Autism Spectrum Disorder, and Relates to Social Communication Abilities." *Journal of Autism and Developmental Disorders* 48, no. 8 (2018): 2653-2662. https://doi.org/10.1007/s10803-018-3515-z.

Henderson, A., and K. L. Mapp. *A New Wave of Evidence: The Impact of School, Family, and Community Connections on Student Achievement.* Austin, TX: Southwest Educational Development Laboratory, 2002.

Heyworth, M. "A Manifesto for Allies Adopting an Acceptance Approach to Autism." *Reframing Autism*, February 15, 2019. https://reframingautism.org.au/a-manifesto-for-allies-adopting-an-acceptance-approach-to-autism/.

Hodgdon, A. Visual Strategies for Improving Communication: *Practical Supports for School and Home.* Troy, MI: Quirk Roberts Publishing, 1995.

Hunter, A. "Sensory Processing and Self-Regulation." *Smart Occupational Therapy Ltd.*, 2020. https://emergentdivergence.com/2023/05/08/mask-on-mask-off-how-the-common-understanding-of-autistic-masking-is-creating-another-mask/.

Hough, L., J. Bleiweiss, S. Cohen, and Mouzakitis. *Three-Tier Model of Strategies and Supports for the ASD Nest Program.* Unpublished manuscript, 2011.

Hölzel, B. K., S. W. Lazar, T. Gard, Z. Schuman-Olivier, D. R. Vago, and U. Ott. "How Does Mindfulness Meditation Work? Proposing Mechanisms of Action from a Conceptual and Neural Perspective." *Perspectives on Psychological Science* 6, no. 6 (2011): 537–559. https://doi.org/10.1177/1745691611419671.

Hunter, A. "Sensory Processing and Self-Regulation." *Smart Occupational Therapy Ltd.*, 2020. https://emergentdivergence.com/2023/05/08/mask-on-mask-off-how-the-common-understanding-of-autistic-masking-is-creating-another-mask/.

IDEA Sec. 300.39 Special Education. US Department of Education, July 2024. https://sites.ed.gov/idea/regs/b/a/300.39.

Jamal, W., A. Cardinaux, A. J. Haskins, M. Kjelgaard, and P. Sinha. "Reduced Sensory Habituation in Autism and Its Correlation with Behavioral Measures." *Journal of Autism and Developmental Disorders* 51, no. 9 (2020): 3153-3164. https://doi.org/10.1007/s10803-020-04780-1.

Jonsson, O. "Understanding Person-Environment Relationships as Criteria to Support the Operationalization of Universal Designing." *Studies in Health Technology and Informatics* 297 (2022): 12-19. https://doi-org.proxy.library.nyu.edu/10.3233/SHTI220815.

Kern, J. K., M. H. Trivedi, C. R. Garver, B. D. Granneman, A. A. Andrews, J. S. Savla, D. G. Johnson, J. A. Mehta, and J. L. Schroeder. "The Pattern of Sensory Processing Abnormalities in Autism." *Autism* 10, no. 5 (2006): 480-494.

Kluth, P., and P. Schwarz. *Just Give Him the Whale!*. London, England: Paul H. Brookes, 2008.

Koenig, K., B. Pfeiffer, M. Sheppard, L. Henderson, and M. Kinnealey. "Effectiveness of Sensory Integration Interventions in Children with Autism Spectrum Disorders: A Pilot Study." *American Journal of Occupational Therapy* 65, no. 1 (2011): 76-85.

Krueger, A. B. "Experimental Estimates of Education Production Functions." *The Quarterly Journal of Economics* 114, no. 2 (1999): 497-532. https://doi.org/10.1162/003355399556052.

Kuhaneck, H. M., and R. Watling. *Autism: A Comprehensive Occupational Therapy Approach*. 3rd ed. Bethesda, MD: AOTA, 2010.

Laushman, P. "How to Improve Your Empathetic Listening Skills." *Thrive Autism Coaching*, December 14, 2022. https://www.thriveautismcoaching.com/post/how-to-improve-your-empathetic-listening-skills#:~:text=According%20to%20the%20Autistic%20Self.

Liebowitz, C. "I Am Disabled: On Identity-First Versus People-First Language." *The Body Is Not an Apology*, March 12, 2015. https://thebodyisnotanapology.com/magazine/i-am-disabled-on-identity-first-versus-people-first-language/.

Lloyd, M. H., N. J. Kolodziej, and K. M. Brashears. "Classroom Discourse: An Essential Component in Building a Classroom Community." *School Community* 26 (2016): 291-304.

Iyengar, S. S., and M. R. Lepper. "When Choice Is Demotivating: Can One Desire Too Much of a Good Thing?" *Journal of Personality and Social Psychology* 79, no. 6 (2000): 995-1006. https://doi.org/10.1037/0022-3514.79.6.995.

McIntosh, K., C. Sadler, and J. A. Brown. "Kindergarten Reading Skill Level and Change as Risk Factors for Chronic Problem Behavior." *Journal of Positive Behavior Interventions* 14, no. 1 (2012): 17-28.

Milton, D. E. M. "On the Ontological Status of Autism: The 'Double Empathy Problem.'" *Disability & Society* 27, no. 6 (2012): 883-887. https://doi.org/10.1080/09687599.2012.710008.

REFERENCES

Milton, D. "The Double Empathy Problem." *National Autistic Society*, March 2, 2018. https://www.autism.org.uk/advice-and-guidance/professional-practice/double-empathy.

Nason, B. *The Autism Discussion Page on Stress, Anxiety, Shutdowns and Meltdowns – Proactive Strategies for Minimizing Sensory, Social and Emotional Overload*. London, UK: Jessica Kingsley, 2019.

National Research Council. *Educating Children with Autism*. Committee on Educational Interventions for Children with Autism, eds. Catherine Lord and James P. McGee. Division of Behavioral and Social Sciences and Education. Washington, DC: National Academy Press, 2001.

New York City Department of Education. *New York City Class Size Report*. Updated February 2023. https://infohub.nyced.org/docs/default-source/default-document-library/2022-23-updated-class-size-report.pdf.

New York State Education Department. *Continuum of Special Education Services for School-Age Students with Disabilities*. Albany, NY: Author, June 2024. https://www.nysed.gov/special-education/continuum-special-education-services-school-age-students-disabilities.

Nowell, S. W., L. R. Watson, B. Boyd, and L. G. Klinger. "Efficacy Study of a Social Communication and Self-Regulation Intervention for School-Age Children with Autism Spectrum Disorder: A Randomized Controlled Trial." *Language, Speech, and Hearing Services in Schools* 50 (2019): 416-433.

O'Donnell, C. L. "Defining, Conceptualizing, and Measuring Fidelity of Implementation and Its Relationship to Outcomes in K-12 Curriculum Intervention Research." *Review of Educational Research* 78, no. 1 (2008): 33-84.

O'Hara, D. "The Intrinsic Motivation of Richard Ryan and Edward Deci." *American Psychological Association*, December 18, 2017. https://www.apa.org/members/content/intrinsic-motivation.

Passarello, N., V. Tarantino, A. Chirico, D. Menghini, F. Costanzo, P. Sorrentino, E. Fucà, O. Gigliotta, F. Alivernini, M. Oliveri, M. Lucidi, S. Vicari, L. Mandolesi, and P. Turriziani. "Sensory Processing Disorders in Children and Adolescents: Taking Stock of Assessment and Novel Therapeutic Tools." *Brain Sciences* 12, no. 11 (2022): 1478. https://doi.org/10.3390/brainsci12111478.

Patten, K. K. "Eleanor Clarke Slagle Lecture—Finding Our Strengths: Recognizing Professional Bias and Interrogating Systems." *American Journal of Occupational Therapy* 76 (2022): 7606150010. https://doi.org/10.5014/ajot.2022.076603.

Pfeiffer, B., M. Kinnealey, C. Reed, and G. Herzberg. "Sensory Modulation and Affective Disorders in Children and Adolescents with Asperger's Disorder." *American Journal of Occupational Therapy* 59, no. 3 (2005): 335-345.

Porges, S. W. *The Pocket Guide to the Polyvagal Theory: The Transformative Power of Feeling Safe*. New York, NY: Norton, 2017.

Prizant, B. *Uniquely Human: Updated and Expanded: A Different Way of Seeing Autism*. New York, NY: Simon & Schuster, 2022.

Pulrang, A. "Words Matter. And It's Time To Explore the Meaning of 'Ableism.'" *Forbes*, October 25, 2020. https://www.forbes.com/sites/andrewpulrang/2020/10/25/words-matter-and-its-time-to-explore-the-meaning-of-ableism/.

Ridderinkhof, A., E. I. de Bruin, R. Blom, and S. M. Bögels. "Mindfulness-Based Program for Children with Autism Spectrum Disorder and Their Parents: Direct and Long-Term Improvements." *Mindfulness* 9, no. 3 (2018): 773-791. https://doi.org/10.1007/s12671-017-0815-x.

Rogers, S. J. "Evidence-Based Interventions for Language Development in Young Children with Autism." In *Social Communication Development in Autism Spectrum Disorders: Early Identification, Diagnosis, and Intervention*, eds. T. Charman and W. Stone, 143-179. New York, NY: Guilford Press, 2006.

Rose, D. H. "Universal Design for Learning: Deriving Guiding Principles for Networks That Learn." *Journal of Special Education Technology* 16, no. 2 (2001): 66.

Ryan, R. M., and E. L. Deci. "Self-Determination Theory and the Facilitation of Intrinsic Motivation, Social Development, and Well-Being." *American Psychologist* 55, no. 1 (2000): 68-78.

Sedgewick, F., L. Hull, and H. Ellis. *Autism and Masking: How and Why People Do It, and the Impact It Can Have.* London, UK: Jessica Kingsley, 2021.

Shalaby, C. *Troublemakers: Lessons in Freedom From Young Children at School.* New York, NY: The New Press, 2017.

Silvertant, M. "Neurotypical & Neurodivergent | Embrace Autism." *Embrace Autism*, August 13, 2018. https://embrace-autism.com/neurotypical-and-neurodivergent/.

Stillman, W. *Demystifying the Autistic Experience: A Humanistic Introduction for Parents, Caregivers, and Educators.* London, UK: Jessica Kingsley, 2003.

Strain, P. S., and E. H. Bovey. "LEAP: Learning Experiences, an Alternative Program for Preschoolers and Parents." In *Preschool Education Programs for Children with Autism*, eds. J. S. Handelman and S. L. Harris, 249-281. TX: Pro-Ed, 2008.

Sussman, F. *More Than Words: A Parent's Guide to Building Interaction and Language Skills for Children with Autism Spectrum Disorder or Social Communication Difficulties.* 2nd ed. Toronto, Ontario: Hanen Centre, 2012.

Sutton, B. M., A. A. Webster, and M. F. Westerveld. "A Systematic Review of School-Based Interventions Targeting Social Communication Behaviors for Students with Autism." *Autism* 23, no. 2 (2019): 274-286.

Tang, G., K. Gudsnuk, S. H. Kuo, M. L. Cotrina, G. Rosoklija, A. Sosunov, M. S. Sonders, E. Kanter, C. Castagna, A. Yamamoto, Z. Yue, O. Arancio, B. S. Peterson, F. Champagne, A. J. Dwork, J. Goldman, and D. Sulzer. "Loss of Motor-Dependent Macroautophagy Causes Autistic-Like Synaptic Pruning Deficits." *Neuron* 83, no. 5 (2014): 1131-1143. https://doi.org/10.1016/j.neuron.2014.07.040.

The Union of the Physically Impaired Against Segregation and the Disability Alliance. *Fundamental Principles of Disability*. 1978. https://disability-studies.leeds.ac.uk/wp-content/uploads/sites/40/library/UPIAS-fundamental-principles.pdf.

VanDerHeyden, A. M., and M. K. Burns. *Essentials of Response to Intervention.* Hoboken, NJ: Wiley, 2010.

Vermeulen, P. *Autism as Context Blindness.* Shawnee Mission, KS: AAPC, 2012.

Walker, N. "Neurodiversity: Some Basic Terms & Definitions." *Neuroqueer*, 2014. https://neuroqueer.com/neurodiversity-terms-and-definitions/.

Wiggins, L. D., D. L. Robins, R. Bakeman, and L. B. Adamson. "Brief Report: Sensory Abnormalities as Distinguishing Symptoms of Autism Spectrum Disorders in Young Children." *Journal of Autism and Developmental Disorders* 39, no. 7 (2009): 1087-1091.

Williams, Z. "Autistic Suicide and Suicidal Ideation." *Autistic Parents UK*, May 2023. https://www.autisticparentsuk.org/post/autistic-suicide-and-suicidal-ideation.

Wise, S. J. *The Neurodivergent Friendly Workbook of DBT Skills.* Lived Experience Educator, 2022.

REFERENCES

Wong, A. *Disability Visibility: Twenty-First Century Disabled Voices*. New York, NY: Vintage Books, 2020.

Wood, R. C., F. Happe, A. Morrison, and R. Moyse. *Learning from Autistic Teachers*. London, UK: Jessica Kingsley, 2022.

Yellow Ladybugs. *Supporting Autistic Girls and Gender Diverse Youth*. Washington, DC: Yellow Ladybugs {Autism}, 2023. https://www.yellowladybugs.com.au.

Zimmerman, A. "10,000 NYC Students Are Shut Out of Programs for Children with Autism. Adding 160 Seats is a Start." *Chalkbeat*, January 31, 2024. https://www.chalkbeat.org/newyork/2024/01/31/nyc-expands-nest-horizon-aims-progrmmams-for-children-with-autism/

ABOUT THE EDITORS

Shirley Cohen (she/her) earned a PhD in developmental psychology from Teachers College, Columbia University. She worked as a kindergarten and first-grade teacher, a remedial reading teacher, and a teacher of children with autism before becoming a faculty member at Hunter College of the City University of New York (CUNY). Dr. Cohen held numerous roles at the college: Director of the Special Education Development Center of CUNY, Director of the CUNY/NYS Regional Center for Autism Spectrum Disorders, Chair of the Department of Special Education, and Associate Dean and Interim Dean of the Hunter College School of Education. She retired from the College as Professor Emerita in 2011.

Professor Cohen is the author of several books in the area of disability, including *Special People*, Prentice Hall, 1977; *Respite Care*, PRO-Ed, 1985; and *Targeting Autism*, 3rd edition, University of California Press, 2006. She also co-edited the original (2013) edition of *The ASD Nest Model*. Professor Cohen directed numerous city, state, federal, and foundation grants. From 2001 to 2013 she worked with colleagues from New York University and Hunter College to develop the ASD Nest program serving students in NYC public schools.

Allison Graham Brown (she/her) is the Executive Director of the Nest Support Project at New York University (NYU) in the Steinhardt School of Culture, Education, and Human Development. Allison earned a BA in psychology from Ohio State University and an MA in education from NYU. Allison has been a proud member of the Nest community since 2006, beginning as a New York City Public School special education teacher at the first Nest middle school. In 2013, Allison joined the Nest Support Project at NYU and has held numerous roles: Instructional Support Specialist, Director of Professional Development, and Director of the Secondary Education Department. During her tenure she supported the launch of the Nest model in Denmark and led the development of the Nest high school model. Allison has been an adjunct lecturer at Hunter College and NYU.

In her current role as Executive Director, she oversees all project business, partners with school leadership to enhance inclusive practices and deepen understanding of neurodiversity in schools, and leads the Support Team at NYU to enact the project vision of a world that authentically embraces its inherent neurodiversity.

ABOUT THE AUTHORS

Dorothy Siegel (she/her), MPA, was the director of the ASD Nest Support Project at New York University's Steinhardt School of Culture, Education, and Human Development from 2003 through 2018. From 2001 through 2018 she collaborated with the New York City Department of Education and with Professor Shirley Cohen of Hunter College to develop, implement, and replicate the ASD Nest program in dozens of New York City public schools.

Ms. Siegel is a long-time advocate for special education reform. Her work with the New York City public school system in the early 1990s led to the creation of the full-inclusion Integrated Co-Teaching (ICT) model, now used widely throughout the public school system. From 1995 through 2006, she was a senior researcher at New York University's Institute for Education and Social Policy, where she directed studies of the New York City Public School System, including an evaluation of New York City's school-based budgeting initiative; a study of the Chancellor's District, an initiative to improve low-performing schools; and a quantitative study of the contributions of individual high schools to student success. She was also the key consultant for the Institute's 1995 report Focus on Learning: Reorganizing General and Special Education in the New York City Public Schools. Ms. Siegel earned a BA from Smith College, an MMus from Yale University School of Music, and an MPA from NYU's Robert F. Wagner, Jr. School of Public Service.

Brandy Stanfill-Hobbs (she/her), MSEd, is the Director of Consultation at the Nest Support Project. Brandy has a BA in Political Science from Wellesley College and a master's from Hunter College, City University of New York. Brandy taught in New York City Public Schools for eleven years, including seven years as a teacher, cluster, and coach in the Autism Nest program. In her current role as Director of Consultation, Brandy supports the instructional and SDI consultant team in partnering with practitioners to enhance inclusive practices and deepen understanding of neurodiversity in schools.

Brandy facilitates professional development and training for Nest administrators and coaches centered on true inclusion, implementing neurodiversity-affirming practices, equity, celebrating neurodiversity, and strength-based approaches in education. She also provides remote and in-person consultation to Nest leadership and practitioners to enhance their equitable and inclusive practices, deepen their understanding of neurodiversity, and support the implementation of the Autism Nest program. Brandy has been an adjunct lecturer at Hunter College, teaching courses on instructional methods for disabled students, and behavior theory and interventions.

Lauren Melissa Ellzey (she/her), MSLIS, also known by the nom de plume Autienelle, is an autistic self-advocate, author, educator, and activist. Through writing, presenting, and consultation, she highlights the inequitable systems that oppress disabled folks across lines of differences. Her work has crossed paths with NeuroClastic, New York University, Reframing Autism, Cripple Media, AbleZine, Think Inclusive, and the United Nations. Her young adult novels, Boy at the Window, Gimmicks and Glamour, and StreamLine, emphasize the importance of belonging for queer, neurodivergent youth of color. In all, she strives to co-create a society where autistic folks nurture one another as we strive toward authentic inclusion. She holds an MS in Library and Information Science and resides in New York City.

Susan Ehlerman (she/her), MS, CCC-SLP, CMT, is a speech-language pathologist and mindfulness teacher, with a focus on bridging and enriching communication between all neurotypes. Since 2003, she has been the primary developer of the Nest Project's Social Development Intervention (SDI) across grades K–12. Additionally, she co-designed the award-winning Subways Sleuths program, an after-school program for autistic children at the New York Transit Museum that builds engagement through a shared interest in trains; runs a private practice in Northampton, MA; consults with psychologists, schools, universities, museums, and parent programs across the country; and delivers workshops that encourage communication between neurotypical and neurodivergent humans using her framework of the Middleground™. Susan has been a guest lecturer at Hunter College and NYU.

Katie Kirkman (she/her), MSEd, BCBA, MSAS, is an Instructional Support Consultant for the Nest program. She provides consultation services to support educators and designs/delivers professional development to practitioners in the Nest program. She also teaches graduate-level courses on understanding behavior and supporting challenging situations. Katie was an elementary school teacher in New York City schools and worked with students and their families as an in-home behavior specialist for over ten years. As a researcher, her interests include teacher efficacy and parents' co-regulatory interactions with their autistic children. Katie has a continued interest in how to improve the experiences of neurodivergent students in the classroom and beyond!

Kristie Patten (she/her), PhD, OT/L, FAOTA, is a Counselor to the President of New York University and Professor in the Department of Occupational Therapy. Dr. Patten formerly served as the Vice Dean of Academic Affairs at NYU Steinhardt School of Culture, Education, and Human Development. Dr. Patten's research focuses on utilizing a strength-based paradigm, in partnership with stakeholders, to understand the impact of our biases and practices on quality of life and well-being, with a focus on interventions in inclusive settings. Dr. Patten has received over $20 million in external funding for her research and programs. Dr. Patten is the Principal Investigator of the